42 Rules for B2B Social Media Marketing

Learn Proven Strategies and
Field-Tested Tactics through
Real-World Success Stories

**By Michael Procopio,
Peter Spielvogel,
Natascha Thomson**
Foreword by Ray Wang

E-mail: info@superstarpress.com
20660 Stevens Creek Blvd., Suite 210
Cupertino, CA 95014

Published by Super Star Press™, a Happy About® imprint
20660 Stevens Creek Blvd., Suite 210, Cupertino, CA 95014
http://42rules.com

First Printing: November 2012
Paperback ISBN: 978-1-60773-113-9 (1-60773-113-4)
eBook ISBN: 978-1-60773-114-6 (1-60773-114-2)
Place of Publication: Silicon Valley, California, USA
Library of Congress Number: 2012951157

The authors are donating all their royalties to the Khan Academy, an organization committed to providing a free world-class education to anyone anywhere. The publisher is matching their contribution dollar for dollar.

Trademarks

All terms mentioned in this book that are known to be trademarks or service marks have been appropriately capitalized. Happy About®, nor any of its imprints, can attest to the accuracy of this information. Use of a term in this book should not be regarded as affecting the validity of any trademark or service mark.

Warning and Disclaimer

Every effort has been made to make this book as complete and as accurate as possible. The information provided is on an "as is" basis. The author(s), publisher, and its agents assume no responsibility for errors or omissions nor assume liability or responsibility to any person or entity with respect to any loss or damages arising from the use of information contained herein.

Early Praise For This Book!

"This book is a must-read for your staff to learn key B2B social media marketing strategies and fill in knowledge gaps. It provides hands-on advice and real-world use cases, unlike many other books on the topic that talk high-level and leave people wanting. Whether you want to build your brand online or turn your organization into a social business, as an executive, this book is a great resource."
Dave DeWalt, Former CEO and President, McAfee

"While the lines between B2B and B2C are blurring, there are aspects of social media that a B2B marketer must carefully consider and navigate. *42 Rules for B2B Social Media Marketing* provides an insightful GPS for the journey that will benefit both the social media novice and the expert."
Jonathan D. Becher, CMO, SAP

"This book moves B2B social media marketing mountains! The authors have taken the complex world of social media and applied specific best practices for the business-to-business space. It is a must-read; do not leave home without it. Essential for any new or seasoned marketer who needs to excel in this brave new world."
Vanessa DiMauro, CEO, Leader Networks LLC

"For those who still think social media is only for consumer marketing, *42 Rules for B2B Social Media Marketing* is a must-read. Beginning with the basics, the authors then take the reader through familiar territory for B2B marketers, showing how social media can boost awareness, influence the influencers, generate leads, and even train the sales force. Read this book before your competitors do."
Tim Matthews, Senior Director Product Marketing, Symantec

"*42 Rules for B2B Social Media Marketing* solves a basic problem: getting you up to speed on social media marketing very quickly. It explains the "why" and "how" in a concise manner. Just the real deal in making social media work for you and your company from people who are used to running big social media programs in B2B enterprises."
Rick Mans, Social Media Lead, Capgemini

"Finally, a concise, practical guide for B2B social marketing! Most of the social media content and advice available on the web focuses on B2C models; it's often hard to find good B2B content. It's great to have a resource written by actual social media practitioners/leaders who have learned how to successfully navigate the complex channels of B2B social marketing."
Maria Poveromo, Senior Director Social Media, Adobe Systems

"While a lot of books have been written on social media marketing, the authors have truly honed in on the unique needs of the B2B marketer, providing actionable advice on how to effectively reach target audiences. Whether you are just getting started in social media, looking for ways to improve your level of engagement, or need a great reference guide to get your teams up to speed, this book has something for everyone."
Marina Greenwood, Principal, Activa PR

"This book is loaded with real-life examples and written in a concise and "to the point" manner. It is a must-read for anybody leveraging the most important aspect of B2B marketing in today's world—digital marketing. While most books of this nature are written purely at the high-level or from a strategic standpoint, this book is comprehensive in that it also discusses digital marketing tools and how to use them effectively."
Sonja Hickey, Senior Product Marketing Manager, HP

"Finally, someone has brought together best practices for B2B social media in a concise and actionable format. Regardless of whether you're new to social media or an industry veteran, you'll find something new you can start implementing right away. This 42 Rules book has become my new go-to reference guide."
Jonathan Chizick, Vice President, MarketingCamp.org

"I absolutely love the format and content of this book! Finally, an easy-to-reference social media resource for B2B companies without a dedicated marketing agency or department. Each Rule is short and snappy, with how-to suggestions anyone can implement one at a time or as part of a comprehensive program."
René Shimada Siegel, President, High Tech Connect

"The rise of social media, content proliferation and mobile applications has made the life of a B2B Marketer difficult to get their message heard. The good news is that this book serves as a playbook with really smart strategies coupled with practical examples of how B2B marketers can use social media to create and distribute meaningful content to their target audience—the right content, at the right time, in the right channel to the right customer."
Michael Brito, SVP Social Business Planning, Edelman Digital

"Natascha, Peter, and Michael have written a book that cuts through all the noise and offers a straight-forward guide for developing and executing a thoughtful and effective social media strategy. A must-read for B2B marketers looking to improve their knowledge of social media and learn how to do it right."
Shelly Milam, Social Media and Digital Manager, Juniper Networks

"Social marketing advice today is predominantly geared to B2C organizations which are fundamentally different from the B2B world. Yet, we know that business-to-business commerce and interactions can benefit greatly from social business practices, and that B2B organizations can have exponential impacts on the global marketplace. "42 Rules" offers valuable, practical guidance for B2B marketers at all levels. The content is well organized for easy reference, includes quick ideas to implement, and is supported by real-world examples."
Mark Yolton, SVP of Digital, Social and Communities, SAP

"This is the first book I have seen on social media which is really prescriptive and written in simple conversational language. As a product marketer practicing social media, I believe these 42 rules will definitely help me engage more with my audience. A must-read book for product marketers who are practicing or want to practice social media!"
Anand Akela, Director, Product Marketing, Oracle

"Like most things I love enough to recommend, this book is ultra-useful and elegantly simple. These three media experts have crafted the ultimate "how to" for anyone trying to navigate the wild and windy social media space, which B2B marketers absolutely must if they want to build meaningful relationships with customers and their network at large. Buy this insightful rule book for everyone in your enterprise (and hide it from your competitors)."
Barry Feldman, Owner, Feldman Creative

"As a marketing executive, social media is an integral part of my marketing strategy. This book clearly demonstrates how B2B marketing professionals can adapt to the rapidly changing social media landscape. An exceptional resource on how to effectively leverage social media, I plan to buy this book for every member of my team."
Ashish Kuthiala, Head of Product Marketing, Electric Cloud

"Through our museum's varied channels, we are attempting to understand who our audience is, create dialogue, and build community in order to communicate most effectively. We've learned that a consistent voice and responsiveness of the institution results in loyal followers who are eager to share, like, and contribute to the conversation on art and artists. *42 Rules for B2B Social Media Marketing* provides a clear guide for any organization that wants to get closer to their audience."
Jill Katz, Director of Marketing and Communications, Institute of Contemporary Art/University of Pennsylvania

"This is a book written by B2B digital and social media practitioners for B2B digital and social media practitioners; the level of detail and comprehension of the differences—and similarities—between markets is impressive. A must-read for those responsible for digital and social program execution within progressive B2B organizations."
Maggie Fox, Founder and CEO, Social Media Group

"In an era where social marketing has become such a critical component to any company's marketing program, *42 Rules for B2B Social Media Marketing* provides an in-depth perspective on today's most effective social marketing tools, diving into real-life experiences from tenured professionals using the best practices in the field. Be prepared to follow a journey on discussing concrete examples of how these best practices work and why they must be followed. It's refreshing as it is revealing and insightful, especially for marketers looking for cost-effective, scalable tools to help them successfully execute on their social marketing vision."
Rana Salman, Ph.D., VP Business Development, Chasse Consulting: Sales Strategies, Inc.

"B2B marketers have seen the potential in social media and social networks to help build stronger relationships with customers and prospects for years, but not really had a manual for how to achieve that goal. This excellent book helps B2B marketers to understand how social can measurably impact their businesses and customer relationships, how to take lessons from the B2C world and apply them in B2B, and lays a foundation and roadmap for marketers to achieve it. Must-read for any B2B marketers looking to integrate social into their programs."
Jen Evans, Founder and Chief Strategist, Sequentia Environics

"*42 Rules for B2B Social Media Marketing* provides a unique blueprint for B2B marketers in the world where marketing communications has been replaced by customer experience and social media engagement. The book is a comprehensive compendium that offers marketers practical advice on how to master the world of social media marketing using the latest techniques and most recent marketing channels. Whether you are only getting started or already have considerable experience in social media marketing, this book is a valuable reference for all."
Lubor Ptacek, VP Strategic Marketing, OpenText

Epigraph

Thanks to Hugh MacLeod and Jason Korman of Gapingvoid for this cartoon. See more of their work at http://gapingvoid.com.

Dedication

To Kathi, Benjamin, and Scott, who support me in all things.
—Michael

To my wife, for her unconditional love and support.
To my children, who inspire me to try new things.
To my parents, for their motivation to seek and share knowledge.
—Peter

To my loving husband Allan, for being an integral part of this journey.
—Natascha

Acknowledgments

Thanks to our colleagues, who constantly challenge us to embrace new ideas.

Thanks to our management, who enthusiastically supported this project.

Thanks to our customers, who constantly seek new ways to collaborate using social media.

Thanks to "eagle eye" Stephanie for her proofreading skills.

Thanks to Allan for his intelligent edits.

Thanks to Chad Summervill for his expertise and contributions about mobility.

Thanks to Hugh MacLeod and Jason Korman of Gapingvoid for letting us use their cartoon.

And thanks to Mike Shaw, for starting us on this journey.

Special thanks to Laura Lowell, Mitchell Levy, Liz Tadman, and the Happy About team for publishing this book.

And thank you to all our reviewers (in alphabetical order):

Anand Akela, Jonathan Becher, Michael Brito, Jonathan Chizick, Dave DeWalt, Vanessa DiMauro, Jen Evans, Deanne Falcone, Barry Feldman, Maggie Fox, Marina Greenwood, Sonja Hickey, Jill Katz, Ashish Kuthiala, Rick Mans, Albert Maruggi, Tim Matthews, Shelly Milam, Vicki Mion, Petra Neiger, Maria Poveromo, Lubor Ptacek, Laura Ramos, Rana Salman, René Shimada Siegel, Allan Thomson, Ray Wang, Mark Yolton

We would also like to acknowledge the following people for helping to shape our ideas about social media, marketing, or making the book possible (in alphabetical order):

Ardath Albee, Roxanne Alexander, Scott Anderson, Tac Anderson, John Appleby, Paul Argenti, Tom Augenthaler, Jay Baer, John Battelle, Andrew Berman, Kristie Bernard, Charlie Bess, Olivier Blanchard, Dorothéa Bozicolona-Volpe, Susan Bratton, Steve Broback, Chris Brogan, Andy Bryant, Mark Budgell, Denise Burns, Keith Burtis, Heather Caldwell, Susan Caney-Peterson, Chris Capehart, Paul Chaney, C.C. Chapman, Tim Collins, Michael Coulson, Perrine Crampton, Michael Crooks, Mia Dand, Gina Debogovich, Tracy DeDore, Cherie Del

Carlo, Lisa Dennis, Gini Dietrich, Jennifer Dirvianskis, John Dodge, Denise Dubie, Starr Hall Egan, Jeff Edlund, Brian Ellefritz, Sally Falkow, Jason Falls, Michael Fauscette, Kathleen Fetters, Mark Finnern, Laura Fitton, Alex Flagg, Peter Flaschner, Bill Flitter, Mignon C. Fogarty, Joe Fox, Dana Gardner, Susan Getgood, Paul Gillin, Pete Goldin, Sarah Goodall, Francois Gossieaux, Louis Gray, Heidi Groshelle, Carole Gum, Andrew Haeg, Roberta Halliburton, Ann Hanley, Rachel Happe, Chuck Hester, Chris Heuer, Neville Hobson, Jack Holt, Shel Holtz, Kari Homan, Lee Hopkins, Kami Watson Huyse, Shel Israel, Mark Ivey, Joseph Jaffe, Heather James, Sudha Jamthe, Jenna Jantsch, Jeff Jarvis, Roger Jennings, Stephanie Jerris, Mitch Joel, Bob Johnson, Nick Johnson, Kim Kane, Beth Kanter, Tatyana Kanzaveli, Doug Kaye, Heather Kenney, Michael Knuckey, Oliver Kohl, Caroline Kohout, Esteban Kolsky, Michael Krigsman, Arnie Kuenn, Mur Lafferty, Leo Laporte, JD Lasica, Bob LeDrew, Charlene Li, Ravit Lichtenberg-Yekutiel, Trish Liu, Geoff Livingston, Rafal Los, Angela Losasso, Laura Mackey, Lisa B. Marshall, Stephanie Marx, Tom Matys, Jennifer McClure, Justin McCullough, Heidi Miller, Scott Monty, Joanne Moretti, Paul Muller, Christine Mykota, Amber Naslund, Michael Netzley, Sean R. Nicholson, Aslan Noghre-Kar, Margaret Nugent, Karen O'Brien, Kieran O'Connor, Sean O'Driscoll, Peter O'Neill, Tim O'Reilly, Brian Rice, Karen Orton, Jeremiah Owyang, Donna Papacosta, Christopher S. Penn, David Pennell, Michael Phares, Alex Plant, Alex Polishchuk, Marilyn Pratt, Joe Pulizzi, Judy Redman, Jon Reed, Bill Robb, Eric Schwartzman, Robert Scoble, Axela Scordato, David Meerman Scott, Dharmesh Shah, Dorothea Sieber, Heather Sieberg, Scott Sigler, Tom Small, Dora Smith, Mari Smith, Brian Solis, Michael Stelzner, Audrey Stevenson, Bill Sweetman, Rebecca Taylor, Will Taylor, Evo Terra, Claude G. Theoret, David B. Thomas, Joe Thornley, Angie Ting, Mark Tomlinson, Lois Townsend, Gina Trapani, Nancy Uy, Ingeborg van Beusekom, John J. Wall, Jeff Warwick, Alison Watterson, Martin Waxman, Debbie Weil, Zena Weist, Tony "Frosty" Welch, Tim Westergren, Phil Windley, Dan York, Charlotte Ziems, Calvin Zito

—**Michael, Peter, Natascha**

Contents

Foreword by Ray Wang

A confluence of forces in society, technology, environment, economy, and politics has emerged to transform B2B marketing as we know it. Prospects overwhelmed by a barrage of irrelevant content and offers automatically tune out marketing noise. Cold calls go unanswered. Email blasts are unopened. Marketing literature is thrown by the wayside. Traditional marketing techniques face fatigue and continue to fail their marketers.

Compounding marketing fatigue, most prospects already know more about your product than your best sales reps. Prospects have the tools to connect with peers and form their own conclusions in the sales cycle. As marketing and support converge, savvy organizations have discovered that their customers know how to support each other better than their best service reps. In fact, marketing has been turned inside out and outside in. Competitors can read everything about your customers and how well your products and solutions fare in the market. Transparency leaves many enterprises and brands exposed.

Inside the boardroom and executive suite, panic has set in. Leaders used to constructs of one-way communications, hierarchies, and command and control models realize social media in B2B marketing is more than a shift. The corporate culture must evolve as enterprises move from transactional systems to engagement systems.

As the world continues to shift from transaction to engagement, a focus on relevancy and context will emerge. This shift to engagement platforms will transform marketing for the next decade and bring sales and support closer to marketing than ever before. Organizations must relearn how to engage in this new model or risk relevancy.

While some old adages still apply, B2B social media marketing comes with new rules. Organizations and brands must rediscover how to mix social media into marketing efforts, create content for social media, leverage key social media sites, use social media in the sales cycle, and put social media into practice.

Success will require marketers to embrace this change. The new medium comes with new risks and new opportunities. The 42 rules outlined here by Michael, Peter, and Natascha articulate how to succeed in this new paradigm. Consequently, CMOs, marketing professionals, and customer experience leaders should take note of the 42 rules in the design of their B2B social media marketing programs.

R "Ray" Wang
Principal Analyst & CEO
Constellation Research

About Ray Wang

R "Ray" Wang is the Principal Analyst and CEO at Constellation Research, Inc. He's also the author of the popular enterprise software blog "A Software Insider's Point of View." With viewership in the millions of page views a year, his blog provides insight into how disruptive technologies and new business models impact the enterprise. Prior to founding Constellation, he was a founding partner and research analyst for enterprise strategy at Altimeter Group and one of the top analysts at Forrester Research for enterprise strategy.

Ray's blog: http://softwareinsider.org/
Ray's complete bio: http://bit.ly/b2bmkt-f01[1]

---

1. www.constellationrg.com/users/rwang0

We believe the B2B (business-to-business) marketer is underserved by material on social media. For example, many social media conferences are B2C-focused (business-to-consumer) and when people ask questions about B2B they often receive blank looks in response. We, on the other hand, work in Global 2000 companies selling to other Global 2000 companies and that is our primary focus.

The primary difference in enterprise B2B marketing is that the sale is more complex, typically high dollar value, where multiple people need to agree to a purchase and those people have different concerns which need to be addressed during the sales cycle. And, the sales cycle typically runs several months with different stakeholders participating at different points in the process. Unlike selling a piece of consumer electronics, many people can say "no," and the "wow, this is cool" factor is minimized by the many meetings to discuss the purchase. B2B marketers also have a smaller set of social media marketing tactics available than our B2C brethren, and we don't usually have the gratification of generating immediate sales from a great campaign.

When we had our first meeting about writing this book, the first question we asked ourselves was, "who is our audience?" After some debate, we concluded that the primary person is a product marketing professional, campaign marketing professional, product manager or other marketing professional who is familiar with traditional marketing and is now being asked to include social media marketing into their mix. In addition, if you manage one or more of these groups, this book will make you conversant in the strategy and tactics of social media.

We are fortunate to work in environments that encourage risk and experimentation, which gives us the freedom and flexibility to try many social media concepts without worrying too much about the immediate, measurable return.

We are active in social media as marketers, educators and speakers. Current and former colleagues come to us for advice on social media marketing, and we find we have to discuss the same basic concepts over and over.

This is our chance to pay it forward, allow others to learn from our experience and mistakes, and to pass on our best practices. And, perhaps, hand someone this book rather than provide another hour of personal training.

There is already lots of great information available on social media (which we will point you to), but not in a single location, not in short, accessible chunks, and not with so many real-world examples. Busy marketing managers and executives know that social media is important to their success, but they do not have time to read multiple 300-page books on the various disciplines within social media marketing. We chose the 42 Rules series because it has the right balance between covering the topic comprehensively and being an actionable, brief, easy read.

Our goal is for this book to be a training reference for new employees and colleagues just starting to venture into social media marketing. We hope it will quickly make them functional (or at least functionally literate) in social media marketing. For more seasoned social media marketers, this book can fill in gaps or provide a starting point to leverage new social channels.

One final note: social media is in its early days. Things are changing very rapidly. We will cover some "why" along with the "how-to" so that you'll be able to apply the tactics to new social media sites as they become available. You can also follow the book and ask questions at http://bit.ly/b2bmkt-i02.[2]

Let's get started!

---

2. www.B2BSocialMediaMarketingRules.com

How to Use this Book

There are several ways to use this book, depending on your role and comfort with social media.

We wrote this book primarily for the **social media practitioner**, especially for marketing professionals, such as product marketing professionals, campaign marketing professionals, and product managers, tasked with starting or participating in a social media program. You already know marketing, but need to extend your knowledge into the field of social media. Or, you are using one social channel and want to do more but don't feel comfortable.

This book can also provide a background for **marketing managers** or **executives** with responsibility for social media, even if they are not actively involved in it on a day-to-day basis. You will need to understand the vocabulary, strategies, and how to measure the success of your social media programs. You may even take the plunge and start "doing social" yourself.

Look below for your category to see the most efficient way to go through the book and get started.

Marketing professionals new to social media

- Read the entire book.
- Choose a few ways you want to get started in social media and re-read the relevant chapters.
- As you become proficient using one social media channel, think about your goals and review Part III ("Leveraging Key Social Media Channels") to determine what to do next.

Marketing professionals with some social media experience

- Review the Table of Contents.
- Read Rule 4 ("Start with Your Audience") to avoid falling into the trap of jumping into a new social channel without having a plan.
- Think about what you want to accomplish with social media and read the chapters to fill the gaps in your knowledge.

Marketing executives overseeing social media

- Read Part I ("Mixing Social Media into Your Marketing") to review why social media is so important for B2B marketing and to become familiar with the key strategies you'll want to make sure your staff is following.
- Review the Table of Contents to see which areas you want to explore in more detail to meet your organization's business objectives.
- If your role includes building pipeline, read Part V ("Using Social Media in the Sales Cycle").
- If you have a very lean team and plan to use external resources to drive your social media programs, read Rule 41 ("Augment with an Agency").

Other professionals that want to use social media to engage with their customers or partners

- Start with Rule 4 ("Start with Your Audience") and Rule 5 ("Listen First").
- Determine your goals and then review the Table of Contents to determine which chapters will help you reach them.

Part I
Mixing Social Media into Your Marketing

Modern marketing is incomplete without a significant social media component. This section will discuss how to complement your existing marketing environment with the right social elements.

- Rule 1: Rules Are Meant to Be Broken
- Rule 2: Go Social, Now
- Rule 3: B2B Social Media is Different
- Rule 4: Start with Your Audience
- Rule 5: Listen First
- Rule 6: Integrate Social Media into Your Marketing Plan
- Rule 7: Be Consistent

1 Rules Are Meant to Be Broken

Social media means that companies must now accept that they are part of a broader market in which their customers are at the center of the universe.

Up until around the 1500s, most people believed that the earth was the center of the universe and the sun and planets revolved around us. Then came the scientific revolution in which the pioneers of modern astronomy, such as Galileo Galilei, Nicolaus Copernicus, and Johannes Kepler, changed the worldview to our current heliocentric model. The change did not happen overnight. Over a period of time, and with much passionate debate, most people came to accept that the earth orbited the sun and was part of a complex planetary system.

We are at such a revolution point with marketing. Until recently, most companies behaved as if they were at the center of the world and everyone and everything circled around them. Organizations marketed to their customers, prospects, and anyone who would listen, through television, radio, magazines, billboards, online banner ads, and direct mail; channels that provide only one-way, outbound communications. By using them, companies pushed their message out and assumed that everyone listened.

Social media turns this model around. Companies must now accept that they are part of a broader market in which their customers are at the center. Companies realize that they do not even control their own brands anymore; the market does, based on what people say about a brand on and offline. The organization, its partners, and even competitors move in complex and interrelated ways to serve the customer.

Smart companies spend their time listening to the conversations customers are having with each other. This is what social media is really about.

Of course, companies participate in the conversations, pushing out their message strategically through the channels we will discuss in this book. But, the communication is now, at a minimum, two-way. If you plan to continue the old way of doing marketing by using "social media" to just push out your content through blogs, Twitter or Facebook without engaging with customers, please return this book; you don't need it.

If you want to listen to what the masses are saying about your company, brands, products, and people, and how to influence perceptions, then this book will teach you several key rules for participating in the dynamic world of social media.

You do not need to follow all the rules to succeed in your social media program. But, focusing on a few, perfecting your techniques, and iterating will launch you ahead of your competitors—at both a corporate and individual level. The nice thing about social media, although a constant source of irritation for some, is that the environment is changing continuously. New platforms frequently come along that require new marketing techniques, which in turn, evolve into new best practices. For those passionate about marketing, these are exciting days full of creativity and promise.

The best way to stay current and maybe even get ahead is to stay in the game. This book will give you the tools you need to enter the playing field, learn the conventions, and compete effectively.

2

Go Social, Now

Social media gives you the opportunity to show up in buyers' search results and to show up higher than in the past because search engines favor fresh content.

I (Michael) started blogging in 2008. Although there was not much research on social media at the time, there was a lot of discussion in the marketing press. I tried it and it worked. One measure of success talked about, even in 2008, was better search ranking.

Fast forward to today; you've been asked to start doing social media. You hear statements like, "We need to get into social media," or "We need to be on Twitter or Facebook, or *<fill in the social network>*." Why is this so important? Since 2008, a lot of research has been done on the topic. It is not just marketing buzz anymore, the facts are clear:

- If you consider a company's home page as the place you start learning about a company, then search engine results are the new home page. 93% of B2B buyers start their search for a product or service on a search engine,[3] not your website. Correct use of social media gives you the opportunity to show up in their search results and to show up higher than in the past because search engines favor fresh content that social media provides. While you might update your website monthly, you'll post to a blog once or twice a week and Facebook or Twitter once or twice a day.
- A 2009 study on trust shows that 90% of people trust recommendations from known people and only 70% trust brand websites.[4] Social media gives you a chance to be that known person and increase the trust of your brand.

---

3. http://bit.ly/b2bmkt-0200
   blog.marketo.com/blog/2011/08/optimizing-landing-pages
   ---why-testing-is-critical.html

- A social media lead (inbound) comes at a significantly reduced cost compared to leads from traditional outbound channels.[5]
- Social media can humanize your company. It exposes the individuals that are involved in designing, building, and selling products and services. It allows these experts to form relationships with customers and participate in online discussions. Since people buy from people, this is a big plus.
- In June 2011, Google added a per person social component to its search results,[6] which means that if a searcher is "connected" to your company (e.g. following you on Twitter or LinkedIn), you will show up higher *in their personal results* than for someone not connected. For more on how social bookmarking sites influence search, see Rule 32 ("Boost Search Placement with Social Media Optimization").
- 9 out of 10 buyers say that when they're ready to buy, they'll find you—since using social media helps your search engine optimization (SEO) and social media optimization (SMO), you will improve your ability to be found.
- Content marketing is a subset of social media marketing. Recent research by Econsultancy and Adobe found that marketers are more likely to agree than disagree that "content marketing is more important than advertising."[7]

From The 2012 Social Media Marketing Industry Report[8]

- The number one benefit of social media marketing is generating more business exposure (reported 85% of marketers), followed by increasing traffic (69%) and providing marketplace insight (65%).
- 58% of marketers indicated generating leads and developing loyal fans are benefits of social media.
- Those investing a minimum of 6 hours per week in social media marketing saw improvements in search engine rankings. Marketers selling to other businesses were more likely to achieve this benefit (59%) than those selling to consumers (50%).
- 58% of marketers who have been using social media for more than 3 years report it has helped them improve sales.

Social media marketing is very important in B2B marketing. While it sounds like a lot of work, don't despair; in Rule 39 ("Make Social Media Part of Your Job"), we'll show you how to use social media to replace some of your current workload.

---

4. http://bit.ly/b2bmkt-0202
   blog.nielsen.com/nielsenwire/consumer/global-advertising-consumers-trust-real-friends-and-virtual-strangers-the-most/
5. http://bit.ly/b2bmkt-0203
   www.hubspot.com/Portals/53/docs/resellers/reports/state_of_inbound_marketing.pdf
6. http://bit.ly/b2bmkt-0206
   googleblog.blogspot.com/2012/01/search-plus-your-world.html
7. http://bit.ly/b2bmkt-0207
   www.marketingpilgrim.com/2011/07/is-content-marketing-better-than-advertising.html
8. http://bit.ly/b2bmkt-0208
   www.socialmediaexaminer.com/social-media-marketing-industry-report-2012/

3 B2B Social Media is Different

While it is true that in B2B marketing you are selling to people, you are selling to multiple people in very different roles.

Last year, I (Michael) bought a new car and was on a team to select a social media product for work. During the process, I uncovered some of the key differences between the sales cycle in B2B and B2C (business-to-consumer) products, including the use of social media.

A car is the most complex thing I buy in my personal life, and yet it seems very manageable. When buying the car, I did all the research on a few websites, checked with some friends on Facebook, and then finalized my decision with a test drive. My choice was as much emotional as based on facts. Once I picked what I wanted, I just needed to get my better half to okay the purchase. Done.

The social media platform experience was VERY different. This was a corporate decision that involved a group of IT folks, corporate social media people, and social media people from other business units. My business unit alone had four people involved; this is typical of committee purchasing with multiple stakeholders who have very different concerns. My business unit had a very specific feature set that was important to us in the social media product. IT had very specific concerns including security and scalability. The financial team had concerns including vendor viability and pricing. Some members of the team checked the vendors' branded communities and other social sites to see what other users were saying about the products.

While it is true that in B2B marketing you are selling to people, you are selling to multiple people in very different roles. These people want information specific to their role and where they are in the sales cycle. Valuable information takes many different forms. First, you need to convince people why their current solution has problems and quantify the business impact. Then, you can show them a better alternative, ideally in the form of happy customers using your solution (success stories, positive statements on social sites, or case studies). In the early stages, people might want background information about your technology. Later, they will be more concerned about how it fits into their specific environment. Business cases or financial justifications will be used with management first, then to convince the CFO or finance manager.

Another difference between B2B and consumer marketing is the size of your target market. For example, there is a company that sells financial software to Chief Financial Officers (CFO) of the Fortune 500. Their market is only 500 companies. Most mass-market car companies would discontinue a model that only sold 500 units annually.

Some social media sites have higher success rates for B2C than B2B marketing and vice versa. For example, Facebook has been most successful for B2C in terms of lead generation. This is true to a large degree because B2C marketing can provide instant discounts and offers that do not make sense for the sale of complex B2B products to large corporations. This relates to the emotional nature of consumer purchases, e.g. my recent car purchase. Conversely, LinkedIn is one of the most successful sites for B2B social media marketing but is not used much for B2C.

What's common between B2B and B2C marketing is that you must still create and frequently update compelling content, focus on engagement, and interact directly with your audience. The main difference in B2B is that you must think about the overall sales cycle, who is involved, and how to address each individual's needs with the right information at the right time.

4 Start with Your Audience

One of the novice mistakes made in social media marketing is starting with a tool or tactic rather than the people or strategy.

A common mistake that novices make in social media marketing is starting with a channel rather than the target audience. It is much easier to create a Facebook page than to build a comprehensive social media strategy. And, it's much less effective.

In the book *"Groundswell,"* Charlene Li and Josh Bernoff define a path to social media usage known as P.O.S.T.: People, Objective, Strategy, Tactics/Tools.

People: There are two reasons to start with your audience.

1. You need to know where your audience congregates. Survey your customers directly and listen for them on social media channels to find out where they go to get information. I (Michael) survey participants every time I teach a class on B2B social marketing. Of those who have Facebook and LinkedIn accounts, they overwhelmingly split their online lives: professional use of LinkedIn and personal use of Facebook. Hence, if you pick Facebook as the main network for your B2B efforts, you may be disappointed.

2. You must understand the needs of your audience to be able to communicate with them effectively. As David Meerman Scott said in *The New Rules of Marketing and PR*, "Nobody cares about your products and services except you and the others in your organization." He adds that you need to

focus on solving a problem the buyer cares about. A CIO cares about different things than a network manager. But, if the network goes down, then the CIO will care.

Objectives: An objective needs to be quantifiable and time-bound. For example, you could set the goal to use social media to recruit 100 registrations to a webinar by a certain date. Make sure you have the tools to measure your goals; in this case the click-through from the social media channel through to the actual registration.

Strategy: How will you achieve your objectives? The strategy for one of my clients was to "increase the number of people we can talk to directly" to improve loyalty. Make sure you have sufficient resources to execute. If you build a great plan, publicize it heavily throughout your organization, and fail to execute, you will be much worse off than succeeding with a more modest approach that delivers measurable results.

Tactics/Tools: These are the specific social media channels you will use to execute on your strategy. For example, to grow your online community, (1) find questions on LinkedIn groups about your products, (2) ask if you can repost them on your community, (3) post the community URL on the LinkedIn group (to lead people there), and (4) when answered, repost the community URL on the LinkedIn group (now demonstrating that the community is a good place to get answers).

Use Case

My (Michael's) team was launching a new software suite to multiple audiences. The first audience was the primary buyer at the director/manager level. The second audience consisted of the influencers; in this case, the users of the software. The third audience was the CIO as the purchase was large enough to require his involvement.

After identifying the prospects' pain points, our strategy was to create awareness of the brand and to communicate benefits of the software to win the deal.

CIOs are generally difficult to reach, but we found some groups on LinkedIn that attracted this specialized audience. We also used targeted advertising on LinkedIn, focusing on people with CIO and VP job titles.

The director/manager group was split between reading blogs and engaging on LinkedIn and Twitter. We created a matrix with the job title along the top and the social channel down the side. In each box, we wrote what actions we would take to engage.

As a result of these social and other marketing efforts, the launch was a great success.

5 Listen First

If you do nothing else with social media channels, at least listen.

If you do nothing else with social media channels, at least listen. My (Michael's) first tool for listening, which I still use daily, was Google Alerts; it's free.

I started with generic listening, that is, just for the brand name. This can raise some issues if the brand name has multiple meanings. For example, in addition to being the world's largest bookseller, Amazon is also a river and rainforest region. In this case, your alerts may provide some content that does not relate to your specific interests.

Two techniques that help are narrowing keywords and negative keywords. Narrowing adds additional keywords, e.g. "target AND retail" to focus on Target the retailer. Negative keywords are words you do not want in your results. Again, for Amazon, if the river shows up in search results then use "Amazon -river" to weed out references to the Amazon River.

Social media provides information you can use to address customer complaints, learn about the competition, and understand key market or technology trends.

Once you have some experience with listening, you should start listening with purpose.

Listen to customers

- Listen for people talking to you. There is little worse than a customer or prospect trying to get your attention and being ignored. Only one-third of users surveyed said they were contacted by the company after making a complaint on Twitter. Of those who were contacted, 83% said they liked or loved hearing from the company.[9]

- Listen for loyal customers or advocates. Capture these posts, for they are public references for your product. For example, on Twitter you can "favorite" tweets. When people go on your Twitter profile and click the "favorites" link they will see all the complimentary tweets about your products or services that you selected.
- Listen for product or enhancement ideas. For example, "I wish the product could also do..."
- Listen to find dissatisfied customers. Your customer service/support team should already be doing this for you.

Listen to the market

- Listen to what the mainstream media report on your company, competitors, and industry.
- Listen for blog posts on topics in your industry. This gives you a chance to engage in conversation with the authors and their audience, which will also boost your ability to influence others and build your profile as a thought leader.
- Listen to LinkedIn groups where experts share ideas. You want to make sure that your point of view is represented fairly.
- Listen for people who need help in your area of expertise; this is a great way to network and find prospects.
- Listen for the competition to gather competitive intelligence. Your competitor's branded communities are particularly good for this.
- Listen to what the key analysts and influencers in your industry are saying.

There are two types of listening tools.

1. Broad-based tools that listen to everything on the channels they cover and provide you information based on keywords you enter. Some of the free ones are Social Mention, Addictomatic, and People Browser. Radian6, Sysomos and NetBase deliver more functionality, for a fee. Visible, SAS and Autonomy are even more sophisticated fee-based tools.
2. Campaign management tools that help you publish and track content with metrics. These include Awareness Hub, HootSuite and Spredfast.

Pick a few of the free tools or some tools your organization has standardized on and experiment. Within a day, you will likely learn something interesting, maybe even something actionable.

---

9. http://bit.ly/b2bmkt-0501
www.maritzresearch.com/~/media/Files/MaritzResearch/e24/ExecutiveSummary TwitterPoll.ashx

6 Integrate Social Media into Your Marketing Plan

Social media makes it much easier for you to put marketing assets in places where your customers and prospects can find them.

Having spent the past two decades in various marketing roles, I (Peter) have found that starting with a solid marketing plan greatly increases the probability of a successful product launch, awareness campaign, or lead generation program. I generally start with the target audience and our goals and use those parameters to create a detailed plan. Social media does not change this process. It does, however, add some new activities. Social media makes it much easier for you to put marketing assets, which you were creating anyway, in places where your customers and prospects can find them.

Use Case

When I (Peter) create a new marketing asset, such as updating a datasheet to support a new version of a product, I:

- Post a status update with the URL on the relevant LinkedIn page.
- Tweet about it and include a link to the document.
- Blog about the benefits of the new version and include a link to the document.
- Upload it, related presentations, and white papers to SlideShare.
- Start an online discussion about why the new features are relevant to my audience and include a link to the document.
- Monitor existing online conversations and engage, quoting the content.
- Invite key customers to participate in the dialogue on social media.

A new customer success story provides you with lots of great content to leverage on social media. If your customer is doing a webinar to share their positive experience with your product, you can promote it using social media and engage with your online community to determine what they are most interested in learning about.

While traditional marketing assets (datasheets, solution briefs, white papers, slide decks) still play a significant role in the sales process, social media has shifted expectations about how people like to consume content. Now, people expect to find information in easy to digest chunks, in a multitude of formats, including video, and in places where they go to find information already, including search engines.

Marketers often make the mistake of viewing social media in isolation when they really need an integrated marketing plan. In this scenario, a social media strategy supports the overall marketing strategy and is not seen as a detached activity.

For campaigns, social media provides additional channels to reach your audience. In addition to direct marketing via email, traditional mail, and phone, you can put your offers and calls to action on social sites where people in your target market congregate. As with other digital marketing initiatives, you can track which sites, headlines, and offers deliver the best results. When you have to provide the return on investment for the time and money you have been spending on social media, you will have the information you need to create reports, analyze, and optimize your marketing spending.

Also consider doing a podcast (see Rule 11, "Podcasts are Easy") or a video (see Rule 20, "Exploit Video with YouTube"); it can be as simple as a 2-minute white board session recorded with a pocket video camera.

Social media provides an opportunity for dialogue with customers and prospects, enabling you to focus your marketing activities on what matters to them most. You can learn their priorities and challenges, allowing your product managers to fine tune product roadmaps as they learn new information about where their solutions fit into the overall market.

If your sales team is typical, they continually request new campaigns and marketing materials so they have a compelling reason to go talk to their accounts. Since you are building these assets anyway, why not leverage them on social media to build awareness and generate leads? Your credibility as a marketing professional, and probably part of your bonus, depends on it.

Be Consistent

You need standards for blogging and other social media activities that match your corporate tone and style while keeping the individual personalities that make the content unique, interesting, and alive.

Think about the image your company portrays to its customers. What does your brand represent? How do you reinforce this image in every interaction with customers and prospects?

Take two popular athletic shoe companies, Nike and Puma. While both sell sports footwear, they each have a very distinct and quite different personality. Nike aims for the serious athlete; Puma focuses more on the lifestyle consumer. They both spend a great deal of time, money, and effort cultivating their brands—both online and in traditional media. This determines how you feel about their brand when you are exposed to their respective names, logos, and products.

The colors, images, and writing style you use in your corporate communications influence how the public perceives you. In most large organizations, there is a branding group that sets and enforces standards for all marketing activities. In some cases, they review all content that goes onto a company's website, including documents, web pages, and the community framework.

While the branding team generally does not review blogs and other online content, social media must conform to the overall corporate guidelines to reinforce the brand.

You need standards for blogging and other social media activities that match your corporate tone and style while keeping the individual personalities that make the content unique, interesting, and alive.

The standards must apply to video and audio too. Consistency reinforces the brand. Common introductions, conclusions, and video style must match corporate brand—fun, buttoned down, or technical. These may vary somewhat to match different audiences.

The challenge is to align your social media content with your corporate tone while speaking in your own voice, which is critical to building creditability online. And, you must speak in the language of your customers, who do not care about your corporate buzzwords or acronyms. They want clear content that talks about how to solve their problems.

Here are some guidelines to better connect with your audience while staying within your brand parameters:

1. Use your customers' language and vocabulary (this will vary significantly when speaking to people in marketing, finance, or IT).
2. Have your own style. If you are creating social media content, presumably you have some expertise to share with your audience. It could be market knowledge, technical expertise, thought leadership, or great stories and anecdotes. Use your authentic voice, which will be easier to maintain over time than a fake persona.
3. Align with your corporate culture. If your company uses irreverent language and images, don't be too serious. On the other hand, if your company avoids humor, you may need to temper your own comedic side to remain credible and on-brand.
4. If your writing skills are weak, take a class. Put your learning into action through various social media channels. Practice makes perfect.

Consistency matters, regardless of the channel, so consider this when creating your social media plan.

Your company probably has some standard graphics or presentation templates. Pick one of these graphics or your logo as your theme for Twitter, SlideShare, and your Facebook cover. No matter where your audience finds you, your brand will immediately come to mind. Also check if your company has social media guidelines that stipulate the usage of graphics/logos on branded social media accounts.

In B2B, if you are not a household name, social media may be the first way a potential buyer interacts with your brand. Make sure your efforts reinforce what the rest of the marketing organization is doing. If your customer already knows your brand, strengthen their positive perceptions.

Part II
Creating Social Media Content

Like traditional marketing, matching the right content to your audience is essential. This section will highlight some ways to create, package, and deliver your message through social channels.

- Rule 8: Tell Stories
- Rule 9: No Marketing Speak
- Rule 10: Blog Regularly
- Rule 11: Podcasts are Easy
- Rule 12: Add Gamification
- Rule 13: Leverage User-Generated Content
- Rule 14: Curate Content to Reduce Your Workload
- Rule 15: Collaborate Using Wikis
- Rule 16: Think Mobile First

8 Tell Stories

Facts tell while stories sell.

There is an old sales adage: "Facts tell while stories sell." This means, you must engage your audience with memorable and compelling content that they will remember. And, since this book is about social media, you want people to share the content and stories with their friends and colleagues.

What kind of stories can you tell? It depends on what interests your target audience. One common and very successful type of story is how one of your customers solved a business problem using your product or service.

Regardless of the media, format, or vantage point, the story must contain several key elements.

- A brief description of the customer's environment, ideally with a lead character (with some direct quotes from this person, if possible)
- The problem or pain they were facing (preferably in the customer's own words)
- How they solved the problem using your company's offering
- The business results (ideally with some quantifiable success metrics)

There are many ways to tell this story and they all work as long as they contain the story elements above. You can write a blog post that contains all the relevant information. Better yet, your customer can write the blog post on their site, yours, or a suitable community.

Or, you can create a video with similar content. The video can be an elaborately produced, multi-camera interview that mixes stock footage, music, professional voice-over, and branding elements into a highly-polished package. With a more limited budget, you can visit your customer with a video camera (even cell phone will suffice in a pinch), and let them tell their story in their own words. The video can stand alone on YouTube or another video hosting site or you can embed it into your blog. Another method is to record a Skype (or similar) video call.

Of course, there are the old-style corporate success stories or solution briefs that do equally well in capturing the message. However, blogs and videos are much easier to share than a PDF document and are certainly more consumable on a mobile device.

If people like your story, they will tell their friends and colleagues, generally by posting it on Facebook or LinkedIn, or forwarding the link via Twitter, text message, or email. If you can have some key influencers or amplifiers in your industry retell the story, your audience expands exponentially.

Many organizations set out to create a "viral" story or video. Unfortunately, your audience controls what goes viral, not you. You can control the story, script, production, audio, and placement, but not whether or not it goes viral.

The key to storytelling is passion and ownership. The story must be your own. Go talk to customers, find out why they buy from your company, share their excitement, and turn it into a story that excites people and drives action.

Your story can either be informational, to build awareness about your solution, or promotional, with a specific call to action such as downloading a document, registering for a webinar, or attending an event. In either case, make it easy for people to share your content by putting sharing buttons on the appropriate pages in your site.

A colleague asked me (Natascha) if using social media can make boring content exciting. The answer is no! While the presentation format can make a huge difference in its consumption and popularity on different social media channels, the underlying story must be good to gain people's attention.

Whatever your story, make it memorable.

9 No Marketing Speak

Be factual, opinionated or funny. (No marketing speak!)

I (Michael) was onboarding a new blogger and received his first blog post for review. The mistake she made is common among marketing professionals making the jump to social media. He didn't change his writing style from traditional marketing to social media.

Traditional marketing speaks formally and as if the person you are speaking to is your client or customer. The tone for social channels is as if you were sitting at your favorite coffee shop with a friend in your industry, explaining your business or product in casual terms.

The quote on my training slides reads:

Be factual, opinionated, or funny

~~Marketing Speak~~

Here is an example of a red lined post:

Before

What this means to customers:

- Key new features that help automate the rollout and management of cloud infrastructures
- More power capabilities for Managed Service Providers
- Accelerates provisioning of new devices
- GUI based Studio allows customers to develop their own drivers

After

What this means for you:

* It helps you automate the rollout and management of cloud infrastructures
* New features specifically for those of you who are Managed Service Providers
* GUI based Studio allows you to develop your own drivers

There is a whole set of words that have been used so frequently that they have lost their meaning. On *Web Ink Now*, David Meerman Scott listed his linguistic analysis of 388,000 press releases. The top gobbledygook terms were:

1. Next generation
2. Flexible
3. Robust
4. World class
5. Scalable
6. Easy to use
7. Cutting-edge
8. Well-positioned
9. Mission-critical
10. Market-leading

Two recommendations: first, remove all superlatives; second, read what you wrote aloud, preferably to another person. If it sounds unnatural, rewrite it.

Don't give your customers gobbledygook. Use plain language; remember, you are talking to your friends.

10

Blog Regularly

*Blogging is a
great way to
start a dialogue
with your
customers,
prospects,
partners, and
fellow
employees.*

It all started with a press release to announce the launch of a new product. Then the press release shrank to a paragraph in a broader corporate announcement tied to a trade show. Then it shrank to a sentence that skipped all the key differentiators about the new product. In other words, the key message was lost and its impact was negligible.

For the marketing executive responsible for the product in question, that was the last straw. He decided it was time to take his message to his target audience himself, unfiltered. That marked the beginning of a blog that ultimately reached the top spot within the company, as measured by page views, for six months straight.

Corporate politics aside, blogging is a great way to start a dialogue with your customers, prospects, partners, and fellow employees. My (Peter's) team started a blog on our system management solutions, which includes roughly a dozen distinct products. The blog gave us the ability to communicate directly with our audience about new product releases, customer success stories, white papers, analysis of industry trends, and technical tips for getting the most value from their investment in our products. We also used the blog to promote events such as speaking engagements, webinars, and trade shows.

The key to a successful blog is great content and compelling stories (see Rule 8, "Tell Stories"). You must provide valuable information on a regular basis to keep your audience interested and coming back. As with most marketing, content is king.

To get started, I recommend you write the titles or abstracts of ten items you would like to post on your blog. Then fully write five of them. At this point, you will have a solid start so you can push out your content on a regular basis and not get stuck having to think and write under deadline pressure. Once you get into a regular blogging cadence, when you come across something interesting, you will automatically think "this would be great for the blog."

Creating a popular blog does not need to take lots of time. We made the blog into a team project. While we had one owner of the high-level editorial calendar, everyone on the team blogged about their own products and the situations they wanted to share with the readers. Each person wrote in their own style, using their own voice. Some authors tended towards technical topics, others towards thought leadership articles. Readers could enjoy the variety of content and the distinct personalities that shine through.

For promoting events or product launches, we generally followed a story arc. The first in the series was a setup of the industry problems. The next focused on the event or product. Post-event, we usually included a summary or transcript of the questions asked at the end, along with the answers and a link to a recording of the event. For product launches, the next post in the series was often a success story about a customer using the product.

Traffic to the blog is not limited to recurring readers checking out the latest post. In fact, most of the page views come from people searching for information on Google about our topic. Because those topics appear in the blog, we showed up high in the results. For this reason, you must write your blog posts with search engine optimization in mind. And then promote your posts through other social channels (see Rule 32, "Boost Search Placement with Social Media Optimization").

The blog can also be a way to leverage existing content. Serialize a white paper, summarize a success story, or repurpose the latest release notes. If you have compelling content, put it on your blog. Great blogs rely on great content and writers with a personality.

Podcasts are Easy

Using audio to deliver content that augments the written word is a great way to engage your audience with a form of multimedia that is relatively easy to create, edit, and share.

I (Peter) was in a meeting with one of my product managers, discussing an upcoming product launch. She had come up with a "top 10" list of reasons to buy the new version of the product. The challenge was how to capture all her passion about this product that she had spent 18 months getting ready for market. The only way we could think of was to use her words along with her voice. Since scheduling a full webinar was not an option (for time and budget reasons), we decided to create a podcast (online audio recording) with the two of us discussing her "top 10" list.

Many people think of podcasts as long content that people download to their phone or audio player for playback later, which sometimes becomes never. (The name "podcast" was derived from Apple's iPod.) You can also create shorter audio segments for your target audience to consume in a streamed format, such as embedded within a blog. We created the "top 10" list to be around five minutes.

Audio is the only format that allows the user to do something else while consuming content. While podcasting shows up low on many surveys (Question: "What information sources do you rely on most?"), recent analysis has shown it is consumed more than average by B2B audiences and the numbers are rising. According to research conducted by Edison Research and Arbitron in May 2012,[10] 1 in 6 people in the USA have listened to a podcast in the last 30 days.

---

10. http://bit.ly/b2bmkt-1101a
    www.slideshare.net/webby2001/the-podcast-con-sumer-2012

Podcasts allow you to provide information in spoken form. Using audio to deliver content that augments the written word is a great way to engage your audience with a form of multimedia that is relatively easy to create, edit, and share in a professional way.

I like to use podcasts to add variety to blog posts (see Rule 10, "Blog Regularly"). You can embed a player on your website or blog so your audio is available with a click of a button. Better yet, you can establish a recurring podcast series to engage with your audience.

The topics you can include in a podcast vary as much as the content in a blog. Since I am not a professional journalist or voice-over expert, I prefer a more casual interview style in which I ask questions of my "guest" about whatever it is we are trying to communicate or promote. This was the format we used when we talked about the "top 10" list of reasons to buy the new product.

Some themes and topics I have used in podcasts include:

- Interview an industry expert about new technology or market trends.
- Interview customers about how they use a product and what business benefits they generate; trade shows are a great venue to find customers to interview.
- Interview a partner company about the synergies of working together.

Creating podcasts is relatively simple. I use a small recording device that records natively to MP3 and has a built-in USB port to upload the files to a computer or website.[11] For editing, I use Audacity,[12] a free digital audio recording and editing program. There are also sites such as TalkShoe.com that provide a conference phone number that records all the participants and provides a convenient audio file you can download afterwards. Some people mix in music to make the podcast sound more professional. I recommend this technique if you have the time and skill to implement it.

Of course, the most important aspect of creating a great podcast is a great script. This doesn't need to be word for word, but everyone should know the questions in advance so they can formulate coherent answers before recording. As with all marketing activities, content is king!

Total cost to get started with podcasting—around $100. What are you waiting for?

---

11. Sony ICD-UX71
12. http://bit.ly/b2bmkt-1102
    audacity.sourceforge.net/

12

Add Gamification

If your target audience is competitive, harness their passion to boost their engagement.

The relatively new field of "gamification" refers to the art and science of increasing people's engagement using techniques from games. The engagement could be with your online community, your products and services, or even other people at a live event.

Many social media platforms draw on people's competitive nature to encourage participation. People receive points or some other virtual currency each time they contribute. Or, they receive special status based on their overall contributions to the community.

At all the large organizations I (Peter) have worked for, every time you post to a blog, start a discussion, or answer someone else's question, you receive some credit. The number of points you accumulate determines your status, which appears next to your name on the site.

For people that are competitive in nature, this system encourages them to participate actively to accumulate points and shed the "novice" or other similar label that is automatically assigned when a person joins an online community. By contributing, they earn points, badges, or status levels; in effect, they earn a reputation.

Airline loyalty programs are one of the classic examples of gamification. Frequent flyers earn "miles" in different ways (flying, credit card, etc.), reach different status levels, and receive perks based on their rank. People would often go out of their way to gain points and the associated bragging rights.

The core principles of gamification include progression, completion, and competition. Let's examine each in the context of social media.

- Progression—the more you participate, the higher your status, which translates to increased credibility and influence
- Completion—closely related to progression, but more tied to milestones or mastery of different tasks
- Competition—a key part of any game that drives people to win

Some companies can harness gamification to boost the effectiveness of a product launch.

Use Case

For example, to recruit more feedback during beta testing for a software testing product, a major vendor asked its beta users to perform various challenges using the software (e.g., report the elapsed time to import 10,000 records). In exchange for each task they completed, they earned points. The person or team that earned the most points won a prize.

As a result of the competitive format of the beta test program, the company attracted four times more participants than the previous "conventional" call for beta testers. And, the number of defects found was significantly higher, due to the more aggressive testing that users did in their quest to earn points.

In addition, the level of engagement on the community site associated with the product was much higher, resulting in increased peer-to-peer learning, a higher volume of discussion around the new version, and better search rankings due to the volume of comments about the software.

Finally, the load on the support organization was lower than usual, even with more people in the beta program. This was due to so many questions being answered by the community. In this case, there is a clear and measurable ROI from using social media.

If your target audience is competitive, harness their passion to boost their engagement with your online community. In your marketing pursuits, encourage your customers and partners to play on the same team.

13 Leverage User-Generated Content

While building a strong online presence using social media is hard work, the fact that it is "social" means you do not need to create all the content yourself. User-generated content takes social media to the next level. In fact, a good collection of user-generated content will make your site more interesting. It will better engage your readers, give them a sense of ownership, and build a stronger community.

There are many different forms of user-generated content, which vary greatly depending on the industry. Here are some examples:

- **News**—BBC News asks its users to provide photos, videos, or commentary on emerging stories where they have some special insight or first-hand knowledge.
- **Product reviews**—Amazon.com asks readers to provide input on their recent purchases. These reviews have become one of the reasons that people visit Amazon.
- **Movie reviews**—Several movie sites accept reviews from their communities and aggregate the results to create a meta-score. Many people find this information from their peers to provide greater value than reviews from professional film critics.
- **Service reviews**—Some companies have built entire businesses around user-generated content. Yelp, for example, lets its members review restaurants, retailers, hotels, doctors and over 20 categories of products and services. The user-generated content is available to anyone, both in aggregate and as the original individual reviews. Furthermore, this content often appears

at the top of search engine results, especially for businesses that do not have an otherwise strong web presence.

- **App store**—Many applications available for mobile devices are created by users. While this content typically uses a different business model for distribution, the owners of the app stores gain publicity and bragging rights for having a rich collection of applications. And, once a person integrates these apps into their daily routine, they are much less likely to change platforms or service providers.

In a typical corporate setting, how you exploit the concept of "user-generated" will depend on your goals and the needs of your users. The key is to find a model that works for you and your audience.

Branded communities (see Rule 23, "Build Branded Communities") are a great way to share user-generated content. This can go way beyond simple discussions about new products and services. Power users can share best practices, templates, scripts, software, drivers, and just about anything relevant for that market. Channel partners can also provide the same content, perhaps giving away some through the community for free and then offering more, or a related professional services component, for a fee.

Calling for user-generated content is a great way to engage your audience. You can ask your customers to write "guest" blog posts. Or, run a video contest where people send in videos of themselves using (or at least talking about) your products. Make it fun.

Use Case

When a high-tech vendor was looking for a way to show that a new version of software offered time-saving improvements, they went to their community. Participants who wrote about their experience with the upgrade received a t-shirt. The community voted on the winner. As a result of this contest, the vendor got over four times the number of submissions they expected—and eventually turned most of these people into formal reference customers. Getting reference customers was traditionally difficult for this vendor; using social media made it easier.

As with most things related to social media, the key to success is setting the right strategy, determining realistic goals, and then getting started with a manageable program; a program for which you have allocated resources to continue until the program proves its value.

14 Curate Content to Reduce Your Workload

Use curation to bolster your social media efforts; you don't have to do it all yourself.

As I (Michael) was reading blogs one day, I found dougmcclure.net where every few posts there would be one titled "Bookmarks for <date>." I didn't realize it until much later, but this was my first exposure to curation.

Curation means selecting and optionally organizing content about a topic. To be useful, the content needs to be of high quality.

The reason curation has become popular in social media is because the amount of social content being created far surpasses anyone's ability to consume it. Having someone pick the best content on a topic is a valuable time saver for the reader, and they will appreciate you for it.

Whatever topic is important to your business probably needs curation. And, you get two large benefits. First, it reduces the need for you to create content. Second, if done well, you will become the trusted source on that topic and your target audience will flock to you.

Use Case

A data center company whose differentiator is being 100% carbon neutral started curating content on green data centers and green IT. By bringing together the best available articles and blog posts about green IT, this company was able to reduce their need to create content to one article per week, even though the site posts multiple articles per day. In addition, they became the recognized experts in green IT and are regularly contacted by the media with questions about green data centers giving them even more visibility.[13]

How to get started

Now that we have (hopefully) convinced you to curate, you are probably wondering how to do it. You can curate content on almost any social platform, blogs, Twitter, Facebook, Pinterest (for pictures), etc.

First, decide where to put the curated content. If your goal is simply to reduce your burden in blogging, create a post on your existing blog with a list or snippets of articles. This is exactly what happened in the doug-mcclure.net example above. ALWAYS include a link to the original post and NEVER copy the whole post; doing so puts you at risk for copyright problems and it is bad form not to give credit (the link) to the originator.

If your goal is to have a site that consists of primarily curated content, the easiest choice is to pick your favorite free blog platform, i.e. Blog-ger.com or Wordpress.com. Then as you see good content on your chosen topic, post it to the blog.

Your company site or a sponsored site?

If you go to GreenDataCenterNews.org, you'll notice that it's not the company's website. Verne Global sponsors Green Data Center News as you can see in the right hand column about one-third of the way down.

Putting a curated site under a separate domain can give it the appear-ance of being impartial and thus more credible. Typically, this type of site has an area listing your company as the sponsor. Having it under your company domain helps drive traffic and search engine optimiza-tion (SEO) for your website. Verne Global could have set up GD-CN.verneglobal.com and reaped the benefit of SEO. The decision on which path to take will depend upon your overall strategy.

Tools to help

There are a range of tools to help curate. You can download free browser plug-in posting tools for many sites. On the other end of the spectrum are complete SaaS (software as a service) solutions where you enter your keywords once, then simply put a tick next to the articles you want displayed. The high end solutions provide a website for you and some, like Curata, will also create and send a newsletter.

Use curation to bolster your social media efforts; you don't have to do it all yourself.

---

13. Example from Pawan Deshpande, founder and CEO of Curata, a curation tool.

Collaborate Using Wikis

On a wiki, any contributor can make changes to the content or format.

Wikis are collaboration platforms that enable the creation, sharing, editing and deleting of information on a hosted site by multiple users. Wikis can be updated ad hoc through a web browser and allow the editing of any contributor's content, not just one's own.

Ward Cunningham, the developer of the first wiki software described a wiki as "the simplest online database that could possibly work."

The most famous wiki is undoubtedly Wikipedia.org. Launched in 2001, Wikipedia has over 21 million articles created by about 100,000 regularly active volunteers. It has become one of the most popular encyclopedias in the world and exists in over 280 languages.

Anyone can add or edit a Wikipedia entry provided they comply with a loose set of policies and guidelines, such as "adding reliable secondary sources." Critics question Wikipedia's accuracy and reliability because it "values consensus over credentials."

Another very popular use of wikis is crowd-sourced software documentation, produced by enthusiastic users. Wikis are inherently very democratic, allowing technical and non-technical users to contribute equally.

Inside corporations, wikis are often used for project collaboration, documentation and to share content. The most common user authorization scenarios are:

- A wiki is open to the public with full public access like Wikipedia.org.

- A wiki is open to the public with restricted access for a limited group of contributors, e.g. they can edit and delete.
- A wiki is enterprise internal-only with access open to the whole corporation but frequently limited to a department or project team.

On a wiki, any contributor can make changes to the content or format, unless a wiki owner has restricted user authorizations. Updates go live immediately. The update history is accessible to provide an audit trail. Regular websites, on the other hand, have fixed formatting that is controlled by a site owner. Content has to go through a publishing workflow that requires approvals before the content can go live. This type of website is unsuitable for real time collaboration.

Wiki tools usually provide capabilities to track recent changes and who made them, revert to a previous version, as well as subscribe to change notifications. This helps the page owner follow any updates and take action against vandalism.

Note: Collaborators on public wikis should be aware of intellectual property rights as they relate to the content that they are publishing.

Use Case

When running the online community video awards for a Global 2000 software company, I (Natascha) had three key collaborators in different locations. We jointly leveraged a wiki on the public community website to announce the awards program, solicit entries, communicate the rules, and share the videos with thousands of members.

The standard wiki formatting options were limited as was my knowledge of HTML. But I was able to copy HTML code from another wiki that had the look I desired and could use on the video competition wiki. My team members were then able to make direct edits to the wiki to improve the formatting further and add content.

Individuals who wanted to enter the contest had to post the URL to their YouTube videos in a designated area on the wiki. Any community member could then comment on the video at the bottom of the page. The system worked well and the program was a crowd-sourcing success.

Wikis are a great tool to enable low-cost team collaboration in an easy-to-use environment. Consider wikis when the ability to make ad hoc changes is critical, shared content does not have to look polished, and an official approval process is not required. You'll be surprised how many people will be interested in sharing their know-how when you make working-together this easy.

16

Think Mobile First

Social marketing was already a fast-moving environment... it has become a NOW environment.

There is a significant chance that the readers of your blogs, tweets and status updates are connecting with you using their mobile devices. In fact, there is a significant chance that you learned about this book through some social platform while browsing on your own mobile device.

However, the device used to engage in social media is only half of the story. Whether I'm on my smart phone, my tablet, or my laptop while sitting at the coffee shop or the airport terminal is of no consequence to my social community. The more important aspect of this evolving marketing platform is the way people are engaging with social tools while they are on the go.

Why mobile?

The latest statistics available from comScore[14] at the time of this writing show a 77% increase in U.S. social engagement from mobile users from 2010 to 2011. More than half of those mobile users connected with social platforms on a daily basis. With the exception of reading and posting status updates for friends, mobile users were most likely to follow links to websites and read information about brands and events.

The social behavior of mobile users creates a huge opportunity for brands and marketers to engage and capture readers, fans, followers, and leads.

---

14. Comscore usage FAQ, http://bit.ly/b2bmkt-1600a
www.cmocouncil.org/resources/docu-
ments/comScore_2012_Mobile_Future_in_Focus.pdf

We offer three simple steps to engage with mobile users:

1. Get on the map. If you have a physical location for your business, get listed on Google and Bing maps to start.[15]
2. Be Check-in Ready. When you exhibit at a tradeshow or have an out-of-store promotion, prepare the location-based services with your information.[16] Have signage at the location asking people to check in.
3. Be ready to respond. Social marketing was already a fast-moving environment. But with the increased usage by mobile users, it has become a NOW environment. When you see a check-in at your booth or physical location, respond with a greeting in real-time.

At the end of the day, B2B social marketing needs to advance your business, which in many cases means lead capture. So, how do you turn mobile users and their social engagement into leads?

1. Consider a "check-in" a cold lead. You can nurture that lead with a greeting and then an offer of more information.
2. Prepare your lead-generation content for mobile users. The stats show that mobile users of social platforms are open to brand content. Be ready to engage with them and make the mobile lead generation experience pleasant. They'll thank you for it by filling out the form.
3. Partner with physical locations around your event to host a meet-up for your social audience. Lead generation is sometimes best done in person.

The other half of the story is the smaller screen size. This impacts text size and navigation; mouse pointers are much smaller than fingers. Make sure you have a mobile version of your site or that it can adapt to mobile screens. Look at LinkedIn.com and m.LinkedIn.com as an example.

When you are creating a new campaign or site, create mobile first.

---

15. http://bit.ly/b2bmkt-1601
    bing.com/businessportal,
    http://bit.ly/b2bmkt-1602
    google.com/placesforbusiness
16. FourSquare, Facebook Check-ins, etc. http://bit.ly/b2bmkt-1603
    foursquare.com/business/merchants/claiming

Part III
Leveraging Key Social Media Channels

You already know all the main social hangouts. This section will cover the best ways to engage your customers through these channels.

- Rule 17: LinkedIn is for Business
- Rule 18: Use Twitter to Broadcast
- Rule 19: SlideShare Builds Awareness
- Rule 20: Exploit Video with YouTube
- Rule 21: Ignore Google+ at Your Own Risk
- Rule 22: Pinterest Creates Referrals
- Rule 23: Build Branded Communities
- Rule 24: Don't Rush to Facebook

17

LinkedIn is for Business

In our opinion, groups should be set up on a topic rather than by company name for marketing.

Over the course of a few B2B campaigns, it became clear to me (Michael) that LinkedIn is a very valuable tool for marketing. As of April 2012, LinkedIn had over 130 million members in 200 countries—with executives from all Fortune 500 companies and more than one million groups.

LinkedIn Groups

LinkedIn Groups are free to set up. However, before starting your own group, we recommend that you look for an existing group on your topic. Recruiting group members is difficult and if someone has already done it for you, why not leverage those efforts?

When I (Michael) started in my first social media position, customers and partners had already established 15 groups with between 300 and 2000 members each that had the company name and/or related technology areas in the group title.

In our opinion, groups should be set up for marketing on a topic rather than by company name. This allows the group to appear vendor agnostic, which will help bring in prospects. Alternatively, you can create both a name-specific and a topic-only group, but this doubles your efforts. By way of comparison, just one of the topic areas covered by one of my products had over 71,000 members. This shows the power of being vendor agnostic.

Like any other community, if you are starting from scratch, expect to have to put a lot of time into building the group. If you can find one already started that has gained traction, it is probably self-sustaining. Also, like any other social media property, you must have valuable content, not just blatant marketing copy. One easy way to avoid "corporate marketing speak" (see Rule 9, "No Marketing Speak") is to use LinkedIn to promote content like your blog posts and webinars. Be judicious with blog posts, perhaps one per week. Asking questions is a great way to get people engaged and to get the community to create content for you (see Rule 13, "Leverage User Generated Content"). Some discussions persist for weeks or months, maintaining the visibility of the person who started the thread.

Polls

LinkedIn Polls are another free tool. You can ask a question and supply up to five multiple choice answers. LinkedIn gives you a URL to the poll as well as an embed code for your blog or website. (An embed code allows you to put the asset from LinkedIn on your web page. Embed codes are also how people put YouTube videos on their websites or blogs.) You can create a string of poll questions, perhaps one per week, to create a small survey. As a vendor, you talk to many customers and can spot potential trends earlier than your average prospect. Using Polls is a good way to confirm your suspicions and provide that valuable content back to the community.

Events

LinkedIn Events is a free place to promote your event. Once you set up the event on LinkedIn, people can find it through search and indicate if they will attend or follow the event. If a person is attending your event, it will show up in their activity stream so that everyone following that person is now exposed to the event.

InMail

LinkedIn InMail is a for fee service. Normally you must be "connected" to a person to send them a message. InMail allows you to bypass that restriction. You will work with the LinkedIn team to select recipients by title, group, location, etc. An InMail comes from a person, so pick a subject matter expert as the sender. In one campaign, there was a 30+ percent open rate and a mid-teen percent click through rate—both far above average.

As you can see, there are a number of ways to use LinkedIn to reach decision makers and match your situation to LinkedIn's capabilities.

18 Use Twitter to Broadcast

Remember there are always folks who know less than you do, so when in doubt, tweet it. One to five tweets per day will keep people watching your account.

In February 2012, Twitter hit 500 million users, according to Twopcharts.com,[17] which gives any message you put out a huge potential reach. Your message will show up in the streams of all your followers and to anyone through search.

The mechanics of signing up for Twitter are easy, but follow the branding advice in Rule 7 ("Be Consistent"). Once you sign up for Twitter, the best way to get followers is to follow people. Search on keywords for your company, industry and product. When you find an interesting tweet, look at the profile of the user. If they look like a person in your target audience or an influencer in your market, follow them.

Twitter started as a text only service and grew to have text based conventions to provide additional functionality.

- @username identifies a user on Twitter; it is how you direct a public message to that user.
- # or hashtag is how you identify a topic in your tweet, for example #socialmedia. If you click on a hashtag in most Twitter clients it will bring up posts on that topic.
- RT stands for ReTweet; use this when you want your followers to see a message from someone you follow.
- DM stands for Direct Message; it is how you send a private message to another user. You can find more information on the Twitter help page.

---

17. http://bit.ly/b2bmkt-1801
    mashable.com/2012/02/22/twitters-500-million-user/

- If you are reading a really interesting article on the web that your target audience would find valuable, tweet the URL with your opinion or insight. Twitter allows for a maximum of 140 characters, though you should only use 120 characters to allow people to retweet without going over the character limit.

Twitter can be used for:

- Broadcasting messages—for example, announcing a new blog post or an event like a webinar.
- Expanding awareness of an event while it is happening by asking people to tweet during the event, using the event hashtag. People talking about your event with the hashtag is a great way to identify people to follow.
- Building relationships—this takes quite a bit of work but it is the most effective use of Twitter. Like in the real world, it requires ongoing engagement to build trust and respect around common areas of interest.
- Finding influencers in your topic area. Once you identify an influencer, you can check their influencer score on a number of services and look at their list of followers to determine if they are a good fit. These people can help to amplify your message on Twitter.

There are many tools that can make the job of managing Twitter easier, particularly if you have multiple accounts, multiple users of an account, or both. HootSuite is a web based, multi-user, multi-account capable tool. Desktop clients are typically multi-account but single user. See Appendix B for a list of tools.

While blogging can be a weekly or twice per month activity, Twitter should be a daily activity. Here's a sample routine for Twitter.

1. Check to see if anyone has mentioned or direct messaged (DM) you at least twice per day. If it is a question, answer it, if not send a thank you or other response to acknowledge receipt. Set Twitter to text or email you when you get a DM.
2. At least once per week, say thanks to any new followers. Review new followers to see if they are worth following. Keep track of your customers and influencers.
3. At least once per month, search for new users as described above.
4. Find a few value-add items to tweet each day.

Repeating the routine above over a whole month takes less than five hours, which provides a pretty good return on your time.

19 SlideShare Builds Awareness

As one of the top 150 sites on the Internet, Slide-Share may be one of the most underutilized resources for businesses to reach decision makers. Here are some additional statistics:

- Over 60 million visitors every month, 14 million registered users[18]
- Has five times more traffic from business owners than other popular websites like LinkedIn, Facebook and Twitter[19]
- SlideShare was recently voted amongst the World's Top 10 tools for education & eLearning[20]

As it sounds, SlideShare.net is a slide (think PowerPoint and Keynote) sharing site. It also allows document and video sharing. SlideShare has free and "pro" accounts. The "pro" accounts are reasonably priced and allow owners to brand the page, remove ads and receive leads (people who view or download the slides).

Use Case

I (Michael) tried SlideShare a few years ago, uploading presentations from a user conference. In one week we had over 4,000 views. Months later we added "lead tracking" and started receiving between 100 and 300 "leads" per month. I put "leads" in quotes because there is no qualification on these contacts other than they

---

18. http://bit.ly/b2bmkt-1911
    blog.slideshare.net/2011/10/04/five-years-of-slideshare/
19. http://bit.ly/b2bmkt-1912
    contently.com/blog/slideshare-content-marketing/
20. http://bit.ly/b2bmkt-1913
    www.slideshare.net/about

showed some interest in the topic. But even with that limitation, you have a group who is self-selecting and can be put into a marketing funnel for more qualification.

Here is our suggestion for getting started with SlideShare:

1. Invest some time looking around SlideShare. Look at your competitors and search on your keywords. Tip—after you get the results from an initial search, SlideShare will give you the option to filter results and search for users.
2. Set up a test account for experimentation.
3. Pay to upgrade to a branded "pro" account and brand it. SlideShare allows you to select a background image. Also fill in all the profile information.
4. Prepare presentations for uploading. SlideShare grabs all the text on the presentation slides AND the notes and puts them in a transcript that shows up after the comments. Unless your notes are for public consumption, remove them or upload as PDF. Make sure you have a call to action in your slides. We end every slide set with a short URL to a landing page or a blog related to the topic. Also consider having Twitter, Facebook, or other account information on the ending slides.
5. Upload the presentation.
6. Fill in metadata; this is very important. Both SlideShare and search engines index the presentations. Your description and tags should be SEO rich. Also select the appropriate category.
7. Manage tags across presentations. Use a common term in the tags for presentations you want grouped together. SlideShare allows you to group presentations in boxes based on tags. We create event tags to group all the presentations given at an event or by a topic. Even if you don't use the box feature, a user can click on any tag and get a list of presentations containing that tag.

Viewers will only have the slide contents to get your message, unless you have put in notes. Another feature of SlideShare is called Slidecast that allows you to play any slide deck synchronized with an audio file you upload. This allows you to provide both the visuals and the explanation to your viewers.

SlideShare is a very effective way to get an audience for presentations, documents, and videos.

20 Exploit Video with YouTube

The goal is not to drive people to YouTube; it is to find people on YouTube and drive them to your website.

Video is one of the fastest growing segments in social media. All your videos should be on YouTube, assuming your videos meet your corporate branding guidelines and YouTube's requirements.

Search is king, even with video

YouTube is the second largest search engine, ahead of Bing and Yahoo, so people are likely to come upon your video when doing a search on a related topic. If your company doesn't have its own video platform, such as Brightcove or Feedroom, also embed your YouTube videos on your corporate website.

The goal is not to drive people to YouTube; it is to find people on YouTube and drive them to your website. To that end, make sure the first thing in the YouTube video description is a URL pointing back to your website. Use a short URL, preferably your own (for example, abcd.com/video1). If getting a short URL is difficult to do in your organization, use bit.ly or a similar shortener that allows you to track clicks.

When you upload your video to YouTube, you will be asked for a title, description, tags, and to pick a category. All of these have important SEO implications, so take some time to select good entries.

YouTube is known for irrelevant and unhelpful comments; however, if you turn them off, you cut off the conversation. We recommend leaving the comments on but monitoring closely or turning on comment moderation.

User experience and marketing

Here are some tips for optimizing your YouTube presence:

- Brand your YouTube channel with look and feel customization. Two examples of acclaimed B2B YouTube channels are KodakB2B and Cisco.[21]
- Pick a good thumbnail. YouTube gives you a choice of the first frame, a frame in the middle, and a last frame. If you can make the first or last frame high impact, you're set. If none of those work, search for "How to set video thumbnails in YouTube" to find out how to make the best use of the system.
- Annotate your video. YouTube annotation provides a lot of flexibility. For example, you can link an annotation to another video or channel on YouTube or a YouTube query. If your video is an interview and a product is mentioned, you can put up the product's name and link it to a search for other videos on the product.
- Use captions and transcripts. Captions are really helpful for non-English speakers; they work the same as closed caption on TV. If you have a transcript of the video, upload it to YouTube. This will further help the SEO of your video. It is also helpful for viewers who read English better than they understand it verbally.
- Participate in the YouTube community, similar to blogging (see Rule 10, "Blog Regularly"), respond to comments and ask for feedback. If you get a good question, create a video to answer it.
- Make sure you allow syndication. Your goal is to get the word out, so unless there is some special reason, perhaps licensed content or someone on the video who doesn't allow syndication, click "yes."
- Finally, market your YouTube channel via other social media channels to get more subscribers. List your YouTube channel on slide decks and wherever you can. The more subscribers you have the more initial exposure you may get, and that may lead to more sharing.

---

21. http://bit.ly/b2bmkt-2001
    www.youtube.com/user/Kodaktube,
    http://bit.ly/b2bmkt-2002
    www.youtube.com/user/cisco

Ignore Google+ at Your Own Risk

What's different about Google+? In some ways nothing...but in other very important ways, it is quite different.

It is early days for Google+, the social network launched by Google in June 2011. As of June 2012, Google+ has over 250 million users, Twitter over 140 million, LinkedIn over 161 million and Facebook over 900 million.[22, 23, 24] In the short time it has been public, Google+ has had significant changes and noticeable impact.

What's different about Google+? In some ways, nothing. Most of the best practices from other networks, especially Facebook, apply: post often, post high quality content, etc. It has the concept of a user and a brand page. But in other very important ways, it is quite different.

Google+ Circles

Circles are the differentiator of Google+. On Facebook you add a friend, on LinkedIn you connect. Once done you need to take special action to limit who can see something you post. On Google+ you put a person or a page in specific "circle(s)." When you post you must select the circle or circles that can see the post. You also have the option to make it public, allowing anyone to see it.

---

22. https://developers.google.com/events/io/
23. http://bit.ly/b2bmkt-2102
    pewinternet.org/Reports/2012/Twitter-Use-2012.aspx
24. http://press.linkedin.com/About

For Google+ pages (think brand page) you can't put someone in a circle until they have put you in a circle, you can't even +Name[25] them in a post. This stops brands from communicating to people who haven't connected to the brand. Facebook has similar restrictions.

Google+ Hangouts

Google+ Hangouts (Hangouts) are a cross between a video conference tool and a webinar tool. Hangouts can be very useful to a marketer.

You can instantly set up a video call or a conference with up to ten people by just clicking the START HANGOUT button, nothing special there. Here's the cool part—you can broadcast your conference call to the world and Google will record it and put the video, as public, on the YouTube channel connected to your G+ account and your G+ stream. You can edit the video on YouTube and republish.

Google+ changes SEO

The reason you shouldn't ignore Google+ is because of Google search. In 2012, Google added "search plus your world" which delivers search results from people you interact with, mostly on Google+. As time goes on, the Google-centric focus may change and results from other social networks may be more balanced, but at this point your SEO will almost certainly be impacted by Google+.

Google is further personalizing search by including what a person's connections talk about. If a person's connections don't "+1" (analogous to "like" on Facebook) or talk about your brand, that person may not see much of your brand and products in Google search results.

Consider that person C likes Canon cameras and person N likes Nikon cameras. They each have a circle called "camera folks." When person C's "camera folks" connections on Google+ do a search on regular Google for cameras, they will see all the posts person C has made, presumably in favor of Canon, even though the posts are not public. The same would be true for person N's "camera folks;" they see all her posts about Nikon.

While Google+ may not offer anything revolutionary in social networking, its large and growing subscriber base and influence on Google search results means you should at least build a presence there and monitor it regularly.

---

25. +Name is a way to refer to a specific person on Google+, similar to the @name on Twitter and Facebook.

22

Pinterest Creates Referrals

The more pictures pinned and repinned, the higher the traffic and SEO effect.

Pinterest has soared out of obscurity to become a top business referral source. As of March 2012, referral traffic from Pinterest was higher than from LinkedIn or Google+, but behind Facebook, StumbleUpon, Google and Twitter.[26]

The basic concept of Pinterest is to create topic boards. You then pin pictures and videos from the web, or upload pictures to your boards. Others can follow you, repin your items to their own board, comment on, or like an item.

This allows users to create online "catalogues" where every picture pinned from your B2B site becomes a referral URL back to your site. Consequently, the more pictures pinned and repinned, the higher the traffic and SEO effect. You can further add URLs and hashtags to the description area of each picture; a must when you upload instead of pin.

The majority of Pinterest users in the USA are women[27] with a relatively high level of education.[28] The most popular topics are: home, arts & crafts, and style/fashion.[29] In the UK, the majority of Pinterest members are male.[30]

---

26. http://bit.ly/b2bmkt-2201
    www.business2community.com/pinterest/pinterest-drives-more-traffic-than-linkedin-and-google-plus-0130492
27. http://bit.ly/b2bmkt-2202
    totalpinterest.com/pinterest-why-its-not-just-for-girls/
28. http://bit.ly/b2bmkt-2203
    www.ignitesocialmedia.com/social-networks/pinterest-demographic-data/
29. http://bit.ly/b2bmkt-2204
    mashable.com/2012/03/12/pinterest-most-popular-categories-boards/

Pinterest is a no-brainer for B2C but how can B2B companies leverage Pinterest best?

For B2B, the best approach is to create boards that convey company culture and values, like sustainability—think solar panels on an office roof—or company volunteering. Consider also posting pictures of what your product might help create, e.g. if it's software, post pictures of the car that gets manufactured using your software. To dazzle on Pinterest, you need crisp and impressive imagery.

A great use of Pinterest for B2B is to create a contest. Ask customers to take a picture with your product and post it with a particular hashtag to their boards, then Tweet or email you the link. The prizewinner could be the person with the most likes for their picture.

A measure of success is when pictures get pinned from your website, repinned, liked and commented on. While a person pinning from your site is already aware of your brand, a repinner might be an untapped opportunity; try to engage this person.

Free tools like Pinpuff and Pinreach provide statistics on followers, likes, repins, influencers, and most popular pins.

While it is unclear if B2B companies will be able to generate revenues from Pinterest in the long run, there is no doubt that the site provides opportunities for businesses to increase brand awareness.

Key tips on using Pinterest for B2B:

- Install the "Pin It" button on your website to encourage visitors to pin. Use pictures in your blogs that can stand alone; also consider creating Infographics and videos.
- Use thisURL: http://pinterest.com/source/<domain>.com to see what has been "pinned" from your and your competitors' site.
- To maximize success, keep pinning and become part of the community. Spread out your posts over several days vs. posting five pictures at once. Follow people and their boards, "like" their pins, and comment.
- Make sure "Hide your Pinterest profile from search" is turned off, but enable publishing to Facebook.
- Apps like "Share As Image" and "Pinstamatic.com" let you pin non-picture content like websites, dates and places.

Keep in mind that copyright laws apply. So don't pin proprietary pictures that you don't own, and watermark your own images. Be aware you are granting broad rights to Pinterest by pinning your content.

---

30. http://bit.ly/b2bmkt-2205
www.webanalyticsworld.net/2012/03/pinterest-usage-and-growth-us-vs-uk.html

23 Build Branded Communities

People will always find ways to engage in online discussions about your company, products, and services, whether you provide the environment or not.

Conversations about your company, products, services, and brand happen every day, both online and offline. The goal is to actively participate in them to develop lasting relationships with your customers. It is impossible to control these discussions, but you can certainly influence them through a branded community.

Branded communities are a great way to engage with your customers, partners, and other interested parties. You can use a branded community to get closer to your customers and promote collaboration by:

- Listening to feedback on your existing products or services
- Learning new ways in which people use your solutions
- Promoting peer-to-peer support in which customers help each other
- Soliciting beta testers and consolidating their feedback
- Sharing information about upcoming offerings
- Opening an online suggestion box

If it sounds like lots of work to set up this infrastructure, monitor it, and respond in a timely manner, you are correct. But, people will always find ways to engage in online discussions (whether on LinkedIn, Facebook, or other discussion forums) about your company, products, and services, whether you provide the environment or not. You will have much more control over your brand and how people perceive it if you provide a somewhat controlled setting for this to happen, rather than being more passive.

A branded community provides a place for facilitated discussions, often called "forums." These discussions are threaded, so people (including your team) can find conversations about specific topics and respond to that particular subject. Many large enterprises have branded communities, often one for each product line to keep the content relevant for the target audience.

One key success factor is ensuring your user base knows about your communities and has good reasons to visit them—rather than seeking information or venting about your products in another forum. Information about your community should accompany every touch point you have with your customers, including product inserts, online documentation, web banner ads, voicemail prompts, newsletters, and emails from sales or service representatives.

Use Case

One technique I (Peter) used successfully to drive traffic to an online community for a software product was to build a sense of urgency by hosting a 24-hour "expert day." This signaled the company's commitment to the community by bringing deep technical resources to answer questions in (near) real time. We had developers, research engineers, product managers, technical marketing, and product marketing people participate in the event, which we started advertising about one month in advance.

The publicity campaign included banner ads on the community itself and related blogs, blog posts three weeks and three days before the event, an email blast to the relevant customers, and mentions by sales and service representatives during phone calls.

In addition to advertising access to information in the existing community, we also made it fun for the employees that participated. We had prizes for the person who answered the most questions and a most valuable player award for the individual who added the most value overall to the day. Every employee that contributed in a meaningful way received a gift card to show appreciation for their commitment to the event. (We used a private employee-only chat room to coordinate responses and locate and assign the proper expert.)

Expert Day doubled the normal participation in the community for that day. We expected this, given the publicity around the event. What was surprising is that the high level of engagement remained at or near that level in the days and months following the event.

If you build an online community, secure commitment from all the stakeholders (business, marketing, and technical) to ensure its success. There is nothing worse than starting a community and then ignoring the people you invited.

24 Don't Rush to Facebook

Facebook is a "fun" place; try things that trigger emotions and joy but still relate to your topic.

When people think of social media, Facebook is often the first thing that comes to mind. For B2B marketing, with its multiple decision makers, there may be better channels to invest your resources.

While Facebook is one of the most popular social networks, members may not be thinking about work while visiting that site. In addition, the person in your target audience must be in the proper mindset to make a corporate purchasing decision. In almost every class I (Michael) teach, I perform a quick survey:

1. Do you have a LinkedIn account?
2. Do you have a Facebook account?
3. Do you split your life into: Facebook for personal use, LinkedIn for work use?

Overwhelmingly I hear YES to question 3. Further, we've done conversion tests by offering discounts to B2B seminars on Facebook, LinkedIn, and Google+. LinkedIn had the highest conversion rate.

Facebook has three constructs, a Profile (personal page), a Page (business page), and a Group (collection of members). Your Profile (timeline) is a complete picture of yourself on Facebook. Pages allow businesses, brands, and celebrities to connect with people on Facebook. Admins can post information and news feed updates to people who like their Pages.

Here are several suggestions for building your company's Facebook Page:

1. Have a complete "About" section; this includes the information that describes your company.
2. Post your terms of participation as a link or on a custom tab. This is insurance in case your page is attacked like Nestle and BP. If you have terms posted, then you can delete posts that are counter to the terms. **Note:** this is not a license to delete all negative posts (see Rule 25, "Etiquette Counts").
3. Post your "office hours" if you are a global company; this way, folks half way around the world will know you are sleeping while they are posting and can come back tomorrow for an answer.
4. Fill in the timeline with milestones in your company history.
5. For most B2B companies, visual items do better than just words, so focus on videos and pictures.
6. Ask questions to foster engagement. It will probably take a while to get "real" people to answer; until then, seed the answer with other employees. Engagement is important because the way Facebook determines which of your posts will show up in people's newsfeeds is in part dictated by engagement with the content.
7. Consider posting items that will eventually lead your audience to a landing page on your corporate site or community. In the end, it is all about leads, even if you are only getting them into a nurturing track.
8. Don't post more than twice per day unless there is something special going on. An email marketing company conducted a survey, and then verified their findings with testing: Twitter users were fine with five posts per day; Facebook users only two per day.
9. Facebook is a "fun" place; try things that trigger emotions and joy but still relate to your topic.
10. Use Facebook Insights to track your progress. Pay special attention to what content is getting the most traction.
11. Use Facebook Ads. In a recent Facebook ad campaign, a company offered discounts to a B2B conference for "liking" its page. This increased their fans per day rate significantly.

Facebook changes the policies and capabilities of their website frequently. You need to keep up with the changes to stay engaged with your customers.

Part IV
Engaging Effectively in Social Media

Social media has its own set of rules, both formal and informal. This section shows how to follow the conventions for maximum business impact.

- Rule 25: Etiquette Counts
- Rule 26: Converse with Your Audience
- Rule 27: Become a Thought Leader
- Rule 28: Use Tools to Manage Channels
- Rule 29: Track ROI Selectively
- Rule 30: Think Global, Act Local
- Rule 31: Influencers Amplify Your Message
- Rule 32: Boost Search Placement with Social Media Optimization

Etiquette Counts

Be yourself, but be yourself at work (not at a bar), chatting with colleagues in a relaxed but professional manner.

Without the usual social cues inherent in face-to-face or even spoken communications, the written word is often misinterpreted. As a result, conventions emerged such as emoticons, use of special characters, or even all caps to convey feelings beyond the text. Your role as a social media professional is to facilitate or engage in (polite) conversation.

If you visit any news site that allows comments, or even YouTube, you can see that things can get very ugly quickly when people hide behind the anonymity of screen names and attack each other, often in deeply personal and very hurtful ways.

Since some people do not follow the rules of online etiquette, many social media sites have built-in ways for their members to self-police. They can "flag" inappropriate content or "vote" comments up or down (or eventually out).

Sometimes this is not enough, and companies use trusted moderators to review all content before it goes live. This requires resources, especially for large and active sites or communities. And this can slow the flow of ideas, possibly limiting the amount of discussion. It is important your company posts its rules for moderation clearly and publicly to avoid the appearance of bias or discrimination when rejecting a post or comment.

The unwritten convention within social media is that companies should avoid deleting blogs or comments unless their content clearly violates one of your status rules e.g., "no discussions on religion and race" or "no use of profanity." There have been some very public (and embarrassing) examples of when companies have removed blog posts they did not like—which tended to amplify the censorship (and resulting bad reputation) by orders of magnitude.

If you are managing a blog or community, here are some tips for encouraging good online behavior:

- Encourage real names to boost accountability. The Wall Street Journal's site does this well and Facebook also requires this.
- Don't delete comments just because you don't agree with them; follow your policy.
- While valid, vigorous disagreement enriches the discussion by serving up different viewpoints, foul language or insults constitute inappropriate content.
- Thank people. Acknowledge their input and content.
- No product or sales pitches and no marketing speak (see Rule 9, "No Marketing Speak").
- Be a person, not a corporation.

If you are participating in online discussions, follow these etiquette guidelines:

- Listen before you "speak." Don't barge into an online conversation without understanding the context.
- In forums, before posting a question, be sure to check if this topic has already been addressed.
- Be yourself, but be yourself at work (not at a bar), chatting with colleagues in a relaxed but professional manner.
- Listen and show that you are engaging to people. Don't just send out generic content.
- Don't overwhelm with too much content all at once. Spread out your posts into digestible pieces.
- Like in a good relationship, listen, then validate before you make a point.
- Before you engage in any social media activity, ask yourself: Would I say the same to somebody's face? Would I feel comfortable seeing it on the front page of a newspaper? If the answer is "no," don't post it.

Frequently, social media posts that are controversial create passionate discussions and engagement. This can be good PR for your business. But if you act boorish to gain attention, it will reflect poorly on you and your company.

While not everybody will agree on what constitutes proper etiquette—particularly in different cultures and countries—you can't go wrong by being polite, respectful, and friendly. As in the face-to-face world, "please" and "thank you" go a long way.

26 Converse with Your Audience

Good marketing depends on being in touch with your target customers. This means knowing what they like, why they buy, how they buy, where they buy, and how your brand makes them feel. Let's say you can meet with 20–25 customers per year. This number could be higher or lower, depending on your specific marketing role. In any case, the real question is: do the customers you meet with in a typical year represent the overall market?

If not, you may have great customer insights, but poor visibility into the overall market requirements. This is especially true if you only meet with your own customers. How do you understand what the people that do not buy from your organization really want? What will it take to expand your market share, and not merely delight your existing customers?

The answer, of course, is social media. Using social media effectively allows you to build and cultivate relationships with buyers, influencers, and thought leaders in your industry. You can use the information you obtain from them to drive product development, build more effective campaigns, refine messaging, and position your company more effectively in the market.

Using social media to establish a dialogue with your customers relies on the typical channels: blogs, LinkedIn, Twitter, community forums, and Facebook—in short, all the places where your customers and prospects spend time online. The key is to listen and participate in the conversations these people are having, sharing your expertise to add value, but injecting your "corporate" opinion only when necessary.

For an effective dialogue through your blogs, respond to comments promptly and politely (see Rule 25, "Etiquette Counts"). Seek out the frequent participants and invite them to share their feedback, either through the blog comments or via direct discussion with the relevant managers or corporate officers.

For Facebook and LinkedIn, monitor what people are saying. You can choose to participate actively if you need to correct factual errors or misstatements, or have information to close knowledge gaps. Many organizations spend much of their time lurking, just to hear what people are saying about their company, products, and services. People tend to speak their minds online (for better or worse), so lurking in discussion groups often provides much valuable information.

For some Twitter comments, it makes sense to post your response to all your followers. Often, you will link to some information that answers a question or clarifies an open issue. For direct messages, reply in the same manner, moving to email or a phone call if the content warrants deeper discussion.

Online communities (see Rule 23, "Build Branded Communities") offer a great forum for building relationships with your customers and establishing a regular dialogue. The key contributors and opinion leaders will make themselves known to the crowd. Be sure to reward those individuals that answer technical questions, freeing up the time of your own team. Badges based on achievement are a common social media currency. Access to corporate insiders or special sneak preview sessions are another great incentive for people who value information.

The key to any of these approaches is to treat people with respect and focus on building long-term relationships. These customers have invested their time and in some cases bet their careers on your company's solutions. Leverage this knowledge and use what you learn from social media channels to guide your marketing activities and prioritize your product development.

27 Become a Thought Leader

Becoming a thought leader is a journey, not a destination.

A common question we hear from colleagues is "How do I use social media to become a thought leader?" First, what is a thought leader? Most definitions hone in on a high level of industry expertise, a willingness to share that knowledge, and the power to influence. In short, it's visibility, backed by capability.

This is very important for marketing, as people looking for solutions will seek expert advice before making purchase decisions. If you or your company appear frequently in search results, people will be steered towards your products or services, even if you do not explicitly discuss them. In fact, if you want to build your credibility as an industry expert, as opposed to a company spokesperson, you are better off not directly promoting your company's wares.

There are several common characteristics of thought leaders. You must be:

- An expert in your chosen field
- Prolific in creating new content that demonstrates your expertise
- Visible (and enjoy the spotlight)
- Sought out by others for your opinions
- Passionate about what you are discussing (if not, who will follow you?)

While social media will not make you a thought leader, you can certainly use it to increase your exposure and build your personal brand (see Bonus Rule 3, "Build Your (Personal) Brand"). However, before embarking on a massive self-promotional campaign, ensure that you really have unique expertise that will be valuable to others. Otherwise, you could, in the best case, be ignored, or in the worst case, destroy your own credibility and perhaps even that of your employer.

Make sure to follow your employer's social media guidelines, which might require you to add a statement such as "opinions are mine and not my employer's" to your social channels. Some companies (especially in highly regulated industries) are more stringent.

If you succeed in establishing yourself as a thought leader, people will put you in the category of influencer (see Rule 31, "Influencers Amplify your Message") and try to gain your favor—inside and outside your organization. Be careful to stay impartial and operate under the modus of "full disclosure," e.g., when you evaluate a customer implementation, or get a free pass to a conference that you write about.

Plan on spending lots of time and effort to learn, network, and gain the wisdom to become a thought leader. Don't risk your reputation by going out before you are ready.

Here are some activities to build your reputation by sharing your knowledge with others using social and traditional channels:

Across all channels, social and traditional
• Stay focused on your chosen area of expertise • Have an opinion and vision • Maintain a consistent presence • Value authenticity and transparency • Focus on integrity and trust—you are your brand • Share information freely • Focus on industry information, business challenges, and trends, not your company's products

"Social"	"Traditional"
• Have a blog • Comment on other blogs • Answer questions online • Speak in webinars • Participate in online discussions (LinkedIn, other relevant communities, Twitter chats, news sites germane to your industry)	• Speak at conferences (promote your engagements online using social media) • Participate on panel discussions • Network with other experts in your field—cooperate, don't compete • Write a column in an influential website or magazine

Becoming a thought leader is a journey, not a destination. Start with the first step.

Use Tools to Manage Channels

The first thing to say about tools is that they come and go, particularly the free ones.

In Part III, we discussed a variety of social media channels, enough to be overwhelming if you try to manage each one individually. This is where the tools come in; they help you save lots of time.

The first thing to say about tools is that they come and go, particularly the free ones. Our primary goal is to give you a sense of what's possible, so that you can find tools with the right capabilities to help your workflow.

Real-time account access

Your smart phone is your real-time friend when it comes to social media. When I (Michael) first started in social media, I had a basic cell phone, so I could only get SMS updates from Twitter. Now that I have a smart phone, which has apps for all the major social media channels, I get real-time updates whenever someone mentions one of the accounts I monitor, including Twitter, LinkedIn, Google+, Pinterest, and Facebook. Having real-time access has transformed the way I monitor social media; I no longer rush to get back to my desk to check on accounts.

Multiple accounts, multiple platforms

An Altimeter study showed that major brands have over 100 social accounts on average.[31] The ability to send and receive messages across multiple accounts in a single application is a

---

31. http://bit.ly/b2bmkt-2801
www.altimetergroup.com/research/reports/a-strategy-for-managing-social-media-proliferation

huge time saver. It is typical today for clients to support Twitter, Facebook, and LinkedIn from a single interface. Many support far more.

I monitor seven Twitter accounts, three Facebook pages and my LinkedIn account with a single tool. The tool (HootSuite) has a tabbed interface and there is one tab for each account.

Multiple users and publishing control

The next challenge, specifically with Twitter, is that each account is connected to only one email address with one password. If I had five people I wanted to share that Twitter account with, I would have to give each of them the password, which presents certain risks. The solution is to have a tool capable of managing multiple accounts connect to each Twitter account. The users each have their own account on the tool and are granted access to the various Twitter, Facebook, or other accounts for which they are allowed to post. This functionality is common on web-based platforms.

An incident with a US auto company in which a person using a multi-account Twitter client accidently sent out a negative tweet on the company account, rather than his own personal account, encouraged some client software companies to add the ability to have a message reviewed prior to being sent out.

Depending on the tool, the user may get a warning to verify a message or there may be author and publisher roles so that only publishers can push the send button.

Other types of tools

In addition to managing messages, there are tools to help track other social media activity, find people with specific attributes, and automate processes. Tools like TwitterFeed and HootSuite accept an RSS feed and convert the feed to tweets. This is really useful for automatically tweeting your blog posts. Each time you publish a blog post, it tweets the title with a link to the post.

Tools like TwitterCounter will provide a graph of the number of Twitter followers you have. Tools like Klout and Kred purport to find influencers. Tweet2Tweet will display tweets as conversations. TweetReach lets you track the reach of up to 50 tweets for free.

As stated earlier, the tools come and go. Put "Twitter tools" or "Facebook tools" or whatever platform into your favorite search engine and you will get lots of articles listing the latest tools. (See Appendix B for a list of tools.)

29 Track ROI Selectively

Measuring the ROI of everything you do in social media takes more time and money than it is worth. Measuring the ROI of specific actions is very doable.

If you initiate almost any social media project, your manager will probably ask you: "What's the ROI (Return on Investment)?" Common responses in social media circles include:

"What is the ROI of the telephone or email?"

"If we take ROI to mean Return on Influence..."

"ROI is easy, of course you can show it."

First, ROI is a financial measure typically expressed as a percentage.

$$ROI\% = \frac{\text{financial return - initial investment}}{\text{initial investment}}$$

Example: I bought 10 apples for $10 and I sold them for $50. ($50*10 apples) - ($10*10) = $400. $400/($10*10 apples) = 4. To get to a percentage = 4*100 = 400% ROI.

For many social media initiatives, both the return and costs are fuzzy. This makes things difficult from a tracking standpoint. I don't believe you can measure the ROI of every action in social media. But you can measure certain *specific* actions.

I (Michael) once measured a 2500% ROI for a lead generation activity with social media. The campaign team was promoting a webinar. Forty-eight hours before the webinar they asked the product manager to:

1. Write a blog post about the webinar.
2. Put a short post on LinkedIn with a link to the blog post.

3. Tweet the link to the blog post.

The return was 100 "leads," that is, 100 people signed up for the webinar. Assume a digital lead costs an average of $40, which would make the return $4,000. In this case, the product manager's burdened cost was $150 for the one hour he spent on the project.

When I told co-workers the results, they immediately challenged them:

- You didn't take into account that he's been building up his blog following over three years.
- You didn't calculate this out for a full year.
- You didn't include all the costs of maintaining the blog.
- Writing a blog post is part of his job.

This is why I only track ROI selectively. Like many other things, the full picture may take more time to calculate than it is worth. But if you bound the problem, it becomes manageable.

The key to obtaining a credible ROI is determining the source of online clicks. For the above example we used a web tracking tool that let us create the links we used in the blog. Then all other activities pointed to the blog. Hence, we could easily report on how many readers clicked the link in the blog to register for the webinar. And how many completed the registration form.

To know which channels are working best for you, create a separate tracking link for each social channel. If you don't have a web reporting tool already set up on your website, you can approximate by using a URL shortening service such as http://bit.ly which will provide statistics on clicks per individual URL. Unfortunately, it only tracks that a person got to a specific page, not whether they completed the form on it. But, you might be able to track this separately.

You also need to design work flow into your campaign to help you track the results as people move through the sales process. One presentation I saw showed how a video was constructed with the goal of getting the viewer to request a demo. The link from the video went to a specific landing page where the viewer could request an in person demo. By tracking those leads through the sales process, the team showed an $8M dollar pipeline increase; they will eventually be able to show the revenue once the sales close.

30 Think Global, Act Local

To participate in social media globally, a business needs qualified resources not only to build and execute a localized strategy, but also to measure and monitor it in the local language.

At the core of successful global marketing is an intimate knowledge of the target audience: their likes, dislikes, customs, and norms.

According to eMarketer,[32] as of December 2011, 1.2 billion people around the world used social media sites at least once a month. China now has the highest number of social media users (about 500 million) and other emerging markets are catching up.

What does this mean for your social media strategy? It means think global but act local. If you are a global corporation or you want to expand internationally, take advantage of the growing adoption of social media around the world to build your brand. But, rely on local experts to guide you.

Being successful globally on social media is not as simple as translating a tweet or a blog into another language. In most cases, local social media requires an understanding of "how the locals tick." For example, Americans tend to be more self-promotional than Germans; Germans perceive it as overly confident and can be put off by it. Hence, while many Americans are happy to share their daily lives, vacations, and successes on Facebook, Germans are less likely to do this in as much detail, as they feel it might come across as bragging. You need to know this to be effective.

---

32. http://bit.ly/b2bmkt-3001
www.emarketer.com/Article.aspx?R=1008870

Consider these points before going global with your social strategy:

1. It's not just about understanding the language; customs, tastes, and interests vary by nation. There is a danger that your message will get "lost in translation" if you don't adjust it accordingly. For example, don't use baseball metaphors for a European audience, or don't try to translate jokes. Listen and learn before you engage, and ideally have local staff or at least regional experts.

2. Rules and regulations vary by country. Do your homework to avoid breaking the local conventions or even the law. In Europe, people are much more concerned about social media privacy than in the US. Being perceived as intrusive can negatively impact your brand.

3. While social media channels like LinkedIn, Twitter, and Facebook are popular globally, they enjoy different levels of popularity in different nations. Many countries have local social media channels in their own language, such as the popular Facebook competitor Renren in China and Orkut in Brazil. Twitter, for example, is not very popular (for business) in Scandinavia, while the Dutch are one of the most active nations on Twitter overall. Don't just rely on LinkedIn, Twitter, or Facebook for your global social media efforts. Do your homework.

4. Have separate social media accounts for each country in which you market. Mixing languages on a single account will cost you followers or fans, as they will get annoyed.

5. Another reason to act local is the adoption cycle. Buyers in emerging economies are often in a different cycle of adoption of a technology than buyers in developed economies. It takes expert know-how to send out the right message to the market or you will miss the audiences' needs and damage your brand.

6. Consumers expect brands that are on social media to be responsive. Make sure you can follow the conversation and engage.

7. Don't make the common mistake of thinking that you have a central marketing strategy that will translate around the world. Social media is all about connecting and engaging; that can only happen when individuals feel validated in their particular interests and needs.

To participate in social media globally, a business needs qualified resources, not only to build and execute a localized strategy, but also to measure and monitor it in the local language. Make sure you have all the pillars in place before taking the journey.

31

Influencers Amplify Your Message

Advocate-Influencers can be great assets when it comes to reaching your social media objectives.

In the age of social media, a new breed of influencers has emerged. The role of traditional influencers has diminished, as the ability to influence has become much more democratic.

Many corporate PR departments have not yet accepted this new reality. Enlightened ones have employed social media to their advantage and started to manage "influencer relations." Analysts no longer hold the same weight as in the recent past. They are part of the old guard who get paid to have an opinion—and they often receive their pay from the companies they evaluate.

Social media has made it possible for anybody to build their own brand by publishing a blog, creating a following on Twitter, or managing a LinkedIn group. And prospects and customers have welcomed these new and independent voices that are often customers themselves. These new influencers establish credibility and trust with high-quality content, candid insights, self-marketing via social media channels, and relationships with other influencers to increase their reach.

Identifying Influencers

Influencers are third parties who understand your space and offering and have a following that respects their opinion and in many cases will act on it. Advocates are ambassadors who understand your offering and are motivated to endorse it; when they are also influencers, you have a powerful force in your favor. There are several tools that claim to identify influence, but they are in the early stages of development. None of them sheds light on motivation; some offer insights into areas of expertise. Klout, PeerIndex, Kred, Trackur, and Twitalyzer, for example, give a score to each tweeter based on their level of activity and network. Other tools like socialmention.com, let you analyze people as to their reach, sentiment, keywords and connections on the Internet, and there are many more similar tools out there.

The main challenge is that no tool exists that can truly measure the quality and strength of relationships. For example, if a person retweets someone frequently, there can be many different motivations. He could have the goal to endear himself to the original Tweeter, he could find the content truly compelling, or he might just want to associate himself with the person and show expertise.

Leveraging Influencers

Influencers can be great assets when it comes to reaching your social media objectives. Provided you understand what they are most interested in and provide them this information via social media, they can amplify your messages to the right people.

Focus on roughly the top 2% of your community as advocate-influencers. Get to know them and build trusting relationships. Find out what motivates them and provide them the information that satisfies their needs as well as helps you meet your objectives.

You have to create a mutually beneficial situation. Never pitch products to an influencer but create opportunities that let them explore your offering or invite them to a demo by somebody they respect.

Ranking Influencers

Consider evaluating your influencers using the following criteria:

Consistency of activities + Consistency of efforts
+ Industry-related conversations and engagement with users
+ Number of followers + Scores from influence measurement tools

---

= Relative influence based on program objectives

Use Case

In Silicon Valley, most large corporations that run successful influencer programs have a hands-on approach. They create exclusive programs for their top influencers, which could be part of "blogger relations." These programs often have resources that provide exclusive benefits to members, e.g., meetings with executives, previews of upcoming technologies, and special access to events.

They also ensure that there is an in-person get-together at least once a year to form close relationships that can then be maintained and leveraged via social media. This is often part of a user conference or other large event.

32
Boost Search Placement with Social Media Optimization

SEO is based on the content and SMO is based on the links to the content.

You have probably heard of Search Engine Optimization (SEO) as a way to boost your placement in search results. Social Media Optimization (SMO) is another way. SEO is based on the content and SMO is based on the links to the content.

With SEO, you build your content and associated metadata around the terms your audience typically uses to search for content. There are specific best practices about how many occurrences of each word and where to place them on your web pages. This discipline has been around for over a decade, so there are many excellent resources on SEO, like SEOmoz.org. Search algorithms change often, which means SEO techniques must also change over time.

SMO has two components:

1. Putting links to your pages or posts on social media sites like Twitter, LinkedIn, and Facebook.
2. Adding the ability to share content on your web pages or posts to social media sites.

When search engines originally came out, they primarily looked at what was on your web page. This determined which search terms would cause your page to appear in the search results. If your page was all about disk drives and had a lot of words about disk drives, you would receive a high rank for those terms.

Then Google entered the picture and brought something new to search. In addition to looking at your page, Google looks to see how many other sites point to your page. The thinking is that each link to your page is a "vote" for your page. The more votes a page gets, the higher it shows up in Google search results.

In addition, the more important the site is that is voting for you, the more "points" you get. If the Wall Street Journal links to your page, you get more "points" than a blog that is infrequently read. Some poorly ranked pages such as "link farms" can even hurt you and take away "points." The length of time a pointing page has been in existence also plays a role in the "point" score. Long-term, credible websites are better than sites recently added specifically to drive web traffic.

Most social media sites are considered "important." Delicious, Facebook, Google+, Reddit, and StumbleUpon, etc. have millions of users and even more viewers—they are "important." As discussed in Rule 21 ("Ignore Google+ at Your Own Risk"), Google+ has special importance for Google searches.

If you use these sites to link to your page or post, you get more "points" in the eyes of the search engines. And the more places people can find a link to your page or post, the higher the chances of it being clicked on.

The other component of SMO is to make your pages "social friendly." Social friendly pages offer tools to share the content on them. This allows others to put the link to your page on a variety of other sites. What if 50 people shared the link to your page or post on Facebook and another 50 shared it on Twitter? That's well over 100 "points" because Facebook and Twitter are "important" sites.

Tools like AddToAny, AddThis, and ShareThis provide one button to get to many of the sites mentioned above and more. As an example, AddThis claims to support over 300 social services and tools supporting over 70 languages and dynamic personalization. If you don't want to use one of these tools, perhaps because of privacy concerns, you can manually put sharing buttons on your page or post.

Being active on social media, adding sharing buttons on your web pages, and encouraging your colleagues and customers to share your content will greatly enhance your company's online presence and visibility.

Part V
Using Social Media in the Sales Cycle

If you are not using social media to drive sales, you are missing one of the most important uses. This section talks about how to use social media to generate leads and grow revenue.

- Rule 33: Build Awareness
- Rule 34: Generate Leads
- Rule 35: Retain Customers and Build Loyalty
- Rule 36: Drive Promotion
- Rule 37: Enable Your Sales Force

33 Build Awareness

Your success depends on knowing the highest-ranking key words and using them in your content and tags so that you can be found.

Awareness creation is one of the most tangible uses of social media. In the tradition of PR, advertising, and broadcast, social media is a great tool to reach the objective of "getting the word out" and building your brand.

The stages to turn a prospect into a customer are: awareness, engagement, and action (see Rule 34, "Generate Leads"). Ideally, this turns into a continuous loop (see Rule 35, "Retain Customers and Build Loyalty") where a customer keeps learning, interacting, buying, and consequently deepening the relationship with your business.

Create Social Media Content to Match Your Customers' Cycle

It's important for your business to have a deep understanding of your customers and their buying cycle. Then, you can offer exactly the right content, to the right person, at the right time.

In the awareness stage, a prospect is generally still trying to understand the full scope of the problem she is trying to solve. This is not the right moment to pitch your product but an opportunity to become a trusted advisor. A blog post on "What to consider when selecting an ERP solution" is a good example of how social media can support awareness. And, of course, you will tweet the blog post (see Rule 18, "Use Twitter to Broadcast").

By providing thought leadership content in the awareness phase, you are able to educate a prospect, gain her trust, and start building a relationship.

The big question is how to get noticed by your target audience. You will often hear that, in the age of pull marketing, the audience will find you if you only provide the right content. But how do you know what the right content is? As a subject matter expert in your field, you need to identify the knowledge gaps that your audience is trying to fill and create content assets that answer their burning questions. One way to do this is by listening to people who are talking about your area of expertise on social media.

Further, as a high percentage of buyers start their journey on search engines, your success depends on knowing the highest-ranking key words (use Google Adwords), and using them in your content and tags so that you can be found (see Rule 32, "Boost Search Placement with Social Media Optimization").

Identify where your target audience goes to get information and engage there. The beauty of social media is that the whole concept is built around people's desires to learn about and collaborate on topics that interest them. For example, there is a vibrant CFO Network group on LinkedIn that discusses topics relevant to CFOs, including software purchases, careers, and market trends.

If you have your own social media channels, use them to deepen awareness of your brand and offerings with existing followers, while at the same time attracting new potential buyers to the community.

Examples of how to use social media to create awareness:

- Write a blog that fills a knowledge gap
- Tweet the URL of a thought-leading white paper
- Answer questions in a relevant forum
- Comment on topical blogs by others
- Create a pin board on Pinterest
- Post a customer success story on Facebook
- Film an educational YouTube video

Measuring the ROI of awareness campaigns can be challenging, as it is often not possible to tie them back to revenue. While specialized software suites are becoming more sophisticated in measuring closed loop marketing, most businesses, even the Global 2000, measure awareness in impressions, views, increase in followers, mentions, and anecdotal evidence.

A key marketing function is to generate leads that ultimately result in revenue.

Some would argue that the primary role of Marketing is to generate leads for Sales. (This opinion would most likely originate from people within the Sales organization). Whether you agree with this premise or not, most people would concur that a key marketing function is to generate leads that ultimately result in revenue for your company.

The rise of social media provides more ways for marketing professionals to reach prospective customers. But, it also comes with a new set of cultural norms that govern behavior through social channels. The penalties for violating these standards are swift, harsh, and often long-lasting. Negative comments, especially as part of an active discussion, will dominate your search results despite your best efforts to displace them. The marketing challenge becomes how to reach your target audience and move them through the sales process without alienating them along the way.

Let's work backwards through the process. To generate a lead, you must somehow capture a person's contact information. This usually comes in the form of an exchange of something that each party values. You provide information that your prospects want and they supply their email address and possibly other information in return.

So, your offer is critical. It must be something that would be difficult or impossible for someone to obtain without giving up their contact information. Webinars fit this framework well, as you need a person's email address to send the registration instructions.

Another high-value asset is a white paper that explains how to solve a business or technical problem your customer or prospect cares about. One challenge here is that since social media rests on the foundation of free information exchange, asking someone to register for a white paper could appear hypocritical. A way around this issue is to serialize the information into a series of blog posts. At the end of each post, you can offer people the opportunity to download all the content in the form of a white paper. This allows your audience to self-select. Some people will opt to download the information for their own convenience in exchange for their email address. Others will prefer to remain anonymous and consume your content spread over several blog posts.

Another factor to consider in making information freely available or not is how many people you want to reach. Locking it behind a registration page may reduce the audience by a factor of 10 or even 100. If you post your white papers openly, be sure to have a call-to-action URL in the document so qualified buyers can find you.

You can and should use social media to drive people to your content. Announce the availability of all your content assets through your blogs, Twitter, LinkedIn, and Facebook. Use these channels to promote your events too.

For optimal lead generation through social media:

- Make it easy for people to contact your company when they are ready to buy. Include links or icons for email, Twitter, Facebook, LinkedIn, and any other channels you monitor.
- Align your landing page to the offer from which it came. If you use certain language in your call to action, mirror that on the landing page to preserve the context.
- Keep your forms simple: name, company, phone, and email. The more fields someone needs to fill out (answering qualifying questions, for example), the more likely they will abandon the form before clicking "submit." Ask for more information over time as you build a relationship.
- Respond quickly to requests for information through the same channel, e.g., LinkedIn messages, direct messages through Twitter, or via email.

Social media provides new ways to capture leads and move them through the sales process.

35 Retain Customers and Build Loyalty

Leverage social channels to lay the groundwork for future cross-sell and up-sell opportunities.

Social media offers many ways to connect with your customers and build loyalty. Every organization knows that the cost of selling to an existing customer is a fraction of the cost of acquiring a new customer, so it makes sense to leverage social channels to lay the groundwork for future cross-sell and up-sell opportunities to your current installed base.

With both marketing programs and relationships, quality matters more than quantity. Having many readers or followers is great, but only if you are listening to customer comments—even when not directed at you—responding to market feedback, and rewarding your most loyal (or profitable) customers.

Here are some ways to build loyalty by engaging with customers through social channels.

- **Respond to issues**—Encourage customers to "follow" your company page on LinkedIn, Facebook, or Twitter. Ask them to join your LinkedIn groups and branded communities. Then, listen to what people are saying about your products, services, and brand. Participating in discussions helps build loyalty because people know you are listening. Develop peer networks that can answer questions about your products and how to use them most effectively. Once a person feels part of a group, they are less likely to leave.
- **Comment on comments**—An active blog or LinkedIn group is a great way to engage with customers and prospects by providing relevant information about the problems your products and services solve. You can start discussions about

new uses for your offering and solicit ideas through comments. Acknowledging a person's comments makes them feel connected to you and your brand.

- **Share information**—For the people that "follow" your company account on Twitter, "like" your Facebook page, or belong to your communities, provide special promotions or early registration codes for webinars or live events. Provide sneak previews of new solutions before you make them available to the general public. Your goal is for people to take the action that will resend your message, broadening its reach to a wider network. Exclusive perks will also make them feel special.
- **Encourage sharing**—Once customers download your app to their phone or tablet, you have now secured a consistent way to reach them with targeted offers. Another way to move customers from loyal to advocates is to create contests that require some level of engagement (such as posting a photo with your product) and encourage them to share their successes and build your brand.

Use Case—Twitter

On one of the Twitter accounts I (Natascha) managed, an industry analyst made a subtly negative comment about a product. Since this was a complex issue, we called her and offered to meet to explain. After the meeting, where we explained we did cover the features she thought were missing, the analyst tweeted that the product did more than she thought.

Use Case—Blogging

One company that I (Peter) worked with helped loyal customers become advocates by offering to let them write guest posts on the company's blog. This was a win-win, the customer increased her public profile and the company received a public recommendation from a user.

Through an ongoing relationship with your customers, you have the opportunity to identify satisfaction issues before they create a social media crisis or cause them to defect to a competitor. You can learn about unmet needs and develop solutions to meet them.

Listening, then engaging is the key to retaining customers and creating loyalty and advocacy.

36 Drive Promotion

Social media extends the value of your marketing machine and expands the reach of campaigns through the power of social networking and search.

Use Case

There was one week left until the webinar and my (Peter's) team only had half the registrations we wanted. We had already posted links on the corporate website and sent emails to our in-house lists. Our media partner had done the same. How could we reach our goal with only five working days until the event? Social media came to the rescue.

"Standard" marketing focuses on putting a compelling offer in front of a targeted audience. Social media extends the value of your marketing machine and expands the reach of campaigns through the power of social networking and search. What were the components of our last-minute push to drive registration for the webinar?

- **Blogging:** We immediately posted details about the webinar (taken from the existing campaign materials) on the blog that related to the webinar topic, along with posts on adjacent solution areas. We changed the first few sentences to target the message and avoid competing for search engine attention. All blogs linked to the registration page. One day before the event, we posted a "last chance to register" item, again with a link to the event. This reached all the regular blog readers and made the content available through search engines.
- **Twitter:** In parallel, we tweeted information about the webinar. We tweeted about once a day during the final week, changing the wording each time to focus on a different aspect of the webinar. Each

tweet included a call to action "learn, hear, see" with a URL to the registration page. This reached all the followers of both our corporate and individual Twitter accounts.

- **LinkedIn:** Each of the presenters posted a status update to their LinkedIn page. Again, they included some short content with a call to action, "On <date> I will be speaking about <topic>. Register at <URL>." The other members of the team also posted to their profiles, with a similar message, "On <date> we are running a webinar about <topic>. Register at <URL>." This reached out to a wide network of all the connections for each presenter.
- **Facebook:** Some of the presenters posted a link to the webinar on their personal Facebook pages; this makes sense if you maintain a single online persona, combining both personal and professional content. Many people use Facebook for friends and LinkedIn for business. In cases where organizations have a fan page for their company, products, or solutions (we did not) it is appropriate to promote a webinar there. All the people in your network or your company's "fans" can see the upcoming event.

For each channel, we used a unique URL and landing page (they all looked the same) to track the source of our registrations. When the big day arrived, we had received over 700 registrations and ultimately over 400 people attended the event.

After the event, we wrote a blog post with a full transcript of all the questions that attendees asked during the webinar, along with our answers. We also included a link to a recording of the event. This blog post provided new value, along with reinforcing the original theme of the webinar and strengthening our position for search engines. As with the original promotional activities, we used Twitter and LinkedIn to build additional awareness about the solution.

In the end, social media helped us reach our goal by driving up registrations and deepening the relationships we had with our audience.

37 Enable Your Sales Force

Social media offers a better way to connect information creators with information consumers.

Sales training or enablement represents one of the most important roles for marketing. In one large technology company, the process followed a one-way, sequential approach from the producer to the consumer. The product marketing managers created content (usually PowerPoint slide decks and perhaps some recorded video training), then went through an elaborate process for posting this onto a portal page. Sales reps (or account executives) could look up what they needed—if they could find it. This arrangement is fairly common in large companies.

Social media offers a better way to connect information creators with information consumers—and ensures that sales reps can find the right information in the right context at the right time.

When my (Peter's) company decided to move to a new sales enablement platform they chose a wiki format. The wiki allowed people to create separate pages for individual sales plays, campaigns, promotions, programs, products, service offerings, solutions, frequently asked questions (FAQs), and competitive analysis. They could build top-level pages that linked to any of the other information. Text, images, audio and video could be embedded, as you would expect in any modern platform or web application.

The biggest benefit of the wiki was the ability for anyone within the company (including the sales team) to contribute or comment on anyone else's information. Errors or omissions were fixed quickly, without having to go through cumbersome and time-consuming processes.

One big inhibitor of permitting anyone to make updates is generally the fear of creating chaos. The key to achieving success in this type of environment is accountability. The wiki platform automatically tracks all changes, who made them, and when. It allows rollback to any prior state. With an individual's credibility and reputation at risk for any misinformation they contribute, everyone tends to be very careful to validate their facts before posting to the wiki.

Other social elements that helped the sales team included the ability for people to rate content and analytics on page views and downloads. When sales reps visited a page for the first time, they could instantly see how many times a video had been viewed and what their peers thought of the content.

While some product marketing people were initially averse to having their materials rated, they soon realized that this mechanism provided valuable feedback and allowed them to prioritize their limited resources on producing only assets that would add the most value to the sales process.

The social features of the wiki also enabled sales to address specific customer needs by forming ad hoc groups around individual issues. Some groups focused on closing a specific deal for a single customer and included account executives, supporting technical or pre-sales resources, and product specialists needed to assist with the sales cycle. Once a deal closed, the group was disbanded. There were groups that contained sales reps focused on a single industry, enabling them to share information about trends, best practices, and successful tactics for meeting unique business needs. These tended to have longer life times, with the membership shifting as people's roles changed through promotion or job transfers.

Use Case

I (Michael) was working a deal with a global bank in New York and put the project materials on the wiki. After completion, I was contacted by a sales person working on a similar project for the same bank, but in Asia Pacific. The sales rep was able to use the New York deal information as a reference. He would never have known of the work I'd done without the benefit of the social platform.

Part VI
Putting Social Media into Practice

As the ancient proverb says, "The journey of 1000 miles begins with a single step." This section provides several actions you can take today to take your social media to the next level.

- Rule 38: Set Goals and Measure
- Rule 39: Make Social Media Part of Your Job
- Rule 40: Start Small and Build
- Rule 41: Augment with an Agency
- Rule 42: These Are My Rules. What Are Yours?

38 Set Goals and Measure

Don't bite off more than you can chew, but experiment and fine-tune before you do more complex things.

Setting clear goals for your social media marketing activities prevents you from spending precious resources without delivering a clear business outcome.

Follow these three steps to define goals that create impact:

Be clear about your business

- Are you planning to become a thought leader in a certain market segment or generate additional revenue? Common objectives are awareness or lead generation. How will you measure success?

Define and locate your target audience

- Who is your target audience? What are their roles and titles? What geography are they in? Are they net new prospects or existing customers? Is your audience in distinct industries or horizontal?
- Identify if each audience requires unique messaging. For example, most business solutions have people who use the product and decision makers who approve the purchase. Very often, these two audiences do not overlap, have different pain points, and get their information from different places.
- Once you understand your target audience, you can identify the right "watering holes" for your social media activity. Watering holes are the places on social media where your audience goes to find information and potentially engage in conversations, e.g., on LinkedIn or Twitter. Your target audience and watering holes dictate what type of content you will need to produce.

Define your marketing and social media goals

- Marketing goals are generally a sub-set of a company's business objectives. Social media goals define how social media is used to support the marketing objectives. Pick just one of your marketing objectives to begin; for example, create thought leadership. Then define metrics to measure success. You may need separate goals and metrics for each channel.
- If you have multiple target audiences, this is the time to decide who you want to focus on first. Especially, if you are just getting started with social media, start small. Don't bite off more than you can chew, but experiment and fine-tune before you do more complex things.

Use Case

I (Natascha) was hired to provide social media consulting for a social media startup. It became clear pretty fast that the company had not set well-defined marketing goals yet. After completing that step, they needed to create personas and clear messaging for each target audience. Social media needed to be part of their integrated marketing plan instead of an isolated program.

The next step was to generate content for each audience that could be used to engage in appropriate social media channels. Fortunately, the company had a number of talented bloggers who were subject matter experts. They initially committed to 2–3 blogs per week to gain traction. After week three, the company was picked up by a Google Alert for the first time.

Creating content, maintaining a corporate Twitter handle, or participating in groups on LinkedIn was a bigger challenge. While it was clear from the marketing goals we defined that all these channels were valid watering holes, there were no resources to manage these channels on an ongoing basis. The client decided to hire a social media manager who could create an editorial calendar for their blog, manage their social media presence, and track metrics. Until the person started, the social media activities were limited to blogging. They tracked blog views and comments, as well as click-throughs from URLs in the blogs to information on their corporate website. So, one success metric might be reducing the cost per click by 30%.

The lesson learned was that one needs to be realistic about the objectives that can be achieved. Make your goals attainable.

39 Make Social Media Part of Your Job

You need to change your processes to make social media part of your job, not an add-on.

As I (Michael) introduced social media to the product management and product marketing teams, they saw it as "one more thing" they didn't have time to fit into their schedule. You need to change your processes to make social media part of your job, not an add-on. Also, at many companies, managers ask their employees to come up with their own performance goals; put social media into your annual or quarterly performance goals.

Here are some examples of how to modify your workflow to make social media a core part of your job.

External Communication

A CEO who started using social media and reduced his conference attendance was chastised by his board of directors. He explained that his job was to communicate. He still went to the most important conferences but found it was more effective to blog than to go to lesser conferences because his message spread further.

Do you spend time writing white papers and eBooks? A white paper could be constructed from a series of blog posts, each blog post could be a table of contents entry. According to Brian Carol, author of "Lead Generation for the Complex Sale," most of the content for his book came from his blog. A book is just a very big white paper.

Are you working with and sending information to influencers such as press and analysts? If your team has cultivated a list of influential bloggers in your industry, simply add them to your contact list.

You've spent considerable time and effort to create the presentations you give to the public. Rather than ask people to email you if they want a copy of the presentation, let them know you put it on SlideShare and ask them to click on "Favorite." This way you won't have as many emails interrupting your workflow and your message will go much farther as others find your content via search.

Research and Testing

If you are doing research, rather than conducting a focus group, use social sites where your customers are talking, such as LinkedIn, Twitter, or your branded community. This works for both product research and message testing. You can just listen, post questions, or use polls.

Are you involved in beta testing? The usual process for running beta tests is for a beta administrator to manage some number of customers testing the product. The admin's job is to solicit feedback from the customers and solve the problems they are having.

One client switched to using a private forum in a branded community for running beta programs. Three advantages came to light.

1. Some customers' questions were answered by other customers. This saved the administrators time and made the customer asking the question happy by getting her answer faster.
2. One administrator could handle more customers because a message could go to all beta testers at the same time rather than one for each customer. Also, common questions only needed to be answered once.
3. By using gamification, the administrators were able to increase the customers' level of testing. Simple tasks like "install the software and post a screen shot of this screen" were presented as "challenges" and customers got points for completing each task.

Marketing job descriptions have changed significantly over the past few years. While the fundamentals of positioning, messaging, lead generation, and branding remain the same, companies are placing higher value on social media skills, mirroring the emphasis the organizations are placing on reaching customers and prospects through these channels.

Start Small and Build

Starting small means mastering one social media channel before moving on to the next.

For many people, anxiety goes along with the thought of using social media. It is no wonder, as the Internet is inundated with blogs that warn of failed social media projects and horror stories of people who struggle to keep up with social media 24/7.

In reality, social media is just another instrument in your marketing tool kit. Like every tool, you have to spend time to learn the basics and then gather real-world experience to apply it most effectively.

There are two schools of thought when it comes to getting started in social media

On one end of the spectrum, social media icon, and ex-Apple evangelist Guy Kawasaki recommends to dive into social media head on and "just do it," as opposed to building a strategy first.[33] Start small in this case means not spending time on developing a social media plan but instead just springing into action.

On the other side, hundreds of social media practitioners and the authors of this book believe that this approach can be dangerous. Getting engaged on social media without understanding the bigger picture can expose a company to many risks. Without a listening strategy, for example, a business might miss negative comments about their brand, an event, or even a direct customer inquiry. In addition, starting in

---

33. Guy Kawasaki: Don't plan your social media, just do it!

one social media channel and subsequently abandoning it, is worse than taking a wait-and-see approach.

Once your business has a social media presence, your customers expect you to respond promptly to their complaints and comments. Make sure you have the resources to staff your social media presence appropriately.

Yes, start small, but by creating your first social media sandbox as a personal vs. a business account. Dive right in, but keep your business out of it while you take the first steps. Of course, this does not work if you are a celebrity or top executive, but you can create a pseudonym account as a sandbox.

How to start small and build effectively

1. Learn in channels others own before starting channels yourself. On Twitter, you have to have an account to participate, but channels like LinkedIn allow you to simply have a profile and participate in others' groups. Leverage this opportunity to learn social media etiquette and protocols.
2. Identify the most promising channel for your social media marketing activity. This is the place where you are most likely to reach your objectives because your target audience is present and engaged in relevant conversations.
3. For the first few days, just listen. Confirm that you are in the right place and learn the dynamics and conventions of the interactions. Imagine you have joined a new club where you don't know any people or even the rules.
4. Identify the rules of successful engagement. Is the expectation that content is polished or free form? SAP Community Network is a mostly technical community and polished marketing content is frowned upon, as it isn't considered genuine. What is valued is original thinking and critical commentary.
5. Attract interest by identifying gaps and providing content to fill it. Instead of pitching a product, provide answers to challenges and pain points expressed by others in the community. This is how you gain trust.
6. Once you feel comfortable, it's time to engage. Answer that LinkedIn question, write that blog, or send that tweet.
7. Clearly define success for each channel. Set metrics and identify tools to track them. Baseline first so you can be realistic.

We have seen many social media projects fail due to over-ambitious plans that could not be executed. Start small, master one channel at a time, then move on to the next, and find success.

41 Augment with an Agency

The combination of internal and external resources usually works best and ensures continuity.

If you are new to social media, it can seem intimidating. This may tempt you to outsource some or all of the responsibility to an external agency. To avoid disappointment, be clear about your objectives, including what competencies you'd like to build in-house vs. outsource long-term.

The most common social media outsourcing scenarios are:

- Listening
- Strategy
- Campaigns
- Execution

Social Media Listening: A listening report can provide insights into your company's share of voice, identify places where relevant conversations are taking place, measure sentiment, and pick up hot topics.

If you decide to buy a license for one of the big social media monitoring tools, keep in mind that you will have to train employees to become experts. Social intelligence tools are complex, have limitations, and require well-trained people to analyze brand sentiment and to come up with actionable insights. This is an area where outsourcing makes sense if an agency has the right expertise. Make sure there is more than one person at the agency (trained) to support your business as this function often sees high turnover.

Social Media Strategy: Outside expertise can add significant value when defining a strategy. But working with an agency requires a considerable commitment on your end, as you are the expert on your business, target audience, and subject matter. You will need to work side by side with a consultant to give direction and make informed decisions. Make sure that the strategy output has clear instructions, milestones, and metrics to ensure you can execute it in a way that will add value to your business.

Social Media Campaigns: Since most marketing campaigns have many inter-related elements, including creative and paid media, it can be very beneficial to hire an agency with the right expertise in this field.

Execution: Many agencies run corporate social media channels for their clients. This requires a streamlined process on how you approve content and pass it on to the agency or you may lose the ad hoc advantage of social media. Also, to respond intelligently to inquiries on social channels, agencies will rely on you and other subject matters experts in your company to provide the answers. Agencies should not be tasked to answer anything but the most basic questions.

Part of the opportunity of social media lies in the ability to establish 1:1 relationships. For example, in a LinkedIn conversation, your goal is to build relationships and establish yourself as a trusted expert. This is difficult, if not impossible, to outsource.

Use Case

In my (Natascha's) personal network of B2B social media professionals, many feel that they've had to "kiss a few frogs" before finding a good agency. Here are some tested tips on what to look out for before signing on the dotted line:

- Many agencies send in their top performer to do the pitch and then designate a different consultant to do the actual work. Don't allow this.
- Have your first meeting in person. After that, it's not necessary to have the resource on-site (agencies might suggest that to make more money).
- Good agencies know your business well. They don't believe that one size fits all but customize their recommendations to fit your needs.
- It is your responsibility to provide them with a 360-degree-view of the situation, access to the platform owners, and brand training.
- Don't outsource your brain. You will have to drive the project and insist on regular checkpoints. The combination of internal and external resources usually works best and ensures continuity.
- Blogger and influencer relations are generally not suited to outsourcing, as the aspect of relationship building is paramount.
- There is agreement in my network that it is all about "the person" and not the agency. It is common that when the trusted consultant leaves the agency, the relationship with the agency ends.

42

These Are My Rules. What Are Yours?

The lines between "traditional marketing" and "social media" are blurring.

A couple of decades ago when you called someone from your cell phone, the conversation probably started with "I'm calling from my cell phone." Perhaps you also went through this phase with your first cordless phone in your home. Now, it's just your phone, with no qualifiers.

We are at such an inflection point in marketing. The lines between "traditional marketing" and "social media" are blurring. Smart companies interact with their customers through a variety of channels, both online and offline. Social media is now mainstream; it won't be long before it's just "marketing."

We have been using social media in our sales, marketing, and product management roles for the past seven years. During that time, the rules have changed significantly. We cannot predict how the online world will look in the next 3–5 years, other than it will be radically different than it is today. Social media will likely play an even more critical role in marketing going forward as mobile computing becomes even more powerful and ubiquitous.

By reading this book, you now have some basic tools to understand the conversations on social media. You know how to listen to the conversations people are having about their needs, challenges, and how happy or not they are with your products and services. You also know the dos and don'ts of engaging in those conversations and starting your own.

It's up to you to use that information to create and market better, faster, and cheaper solutions to increase business value.

Good luck! And follow us on the website http://www.B2BSocialMediaMarketingRules.com, as we update the book online to keep it up-to-date. On this site we will provide updates to the topics in the book to keep you current and answer your questions.

http://www.B2BSocialMediaMarketingRules.com

Bonus Rules

In social media, it seems that most "rules" serve as guidelines, until something changes and there is a new way for collaborating online with your friends, colleagues, customers, and prospects. Here are some more "rules" that we wanted to share.

- Bonus Rule 1: Use LinkedIn for Market Research
- Bonus Rule 2: Make a Good Tweet
- Bonus Rule 3: Build Your (Personal) Brand
- Bonus Rule 4: Use Social Media for Internal Marketing
- Bonus Rule 5: Extend Live Events with Mobile Apps

The only constant with social media is change. To allow this book to keep up with the dynamic subject, we have set up a website, http://bit.ly/b2bmkt-i02.[34] On the site, we will keep you up-to-date on changes that affect the "rules" and perhaps create additional bonus rules.

www.B2BSocialMediaMarketingRules.com

---

34. http://bit.ly/b2bmkt-i02
www.B2BSocialMediaMarketingRules.com

1 Use LinkedIn for Market Research

In three days, I had more volunteers for the research than I had time to interview.

LinkedIn is a great tool for market research. Try it to address the issues below. Some of the 100+ million users probably have the information you are seeking.

Product Research

I (Michael) was researching user needs for a new product. The user persona was a relatively new job title called a problem manager. In speaking with one of the large analyst firms, they told me they had only been able to find ten people. This was not encouraging.

I went to LinkedIn and searched for this job title. LinkedIn displayed ten pages of people with that title, ten contacts per page. I sent messages to four people asking to interview them and received two positive responses within 48 hours.

For a different area in the same product, I needed to determine how existing operations teams solved a specific problem. This time I went to the LinkedIn group on the topic and asked for people to interview. In three days, I had more volunteers for the research than I had time to interview, and they were from around the world—Australia, Germany, UK, and United States.

Messaging Research

An agency was helping us develop a campaign to launch a new product. The basis of the program was around understanding the key performance indicators executives use to measure IT. We needed to make sure what we said would resonate with the intended audience.

The agency went to a LinkedIn group for CEOs and asked our question. The subsequent discussion gave us some of the answers we needed. More importantly, once the product launched we could use that group to get reactions to our positioning and use them as validation and/or tuning for our messaging. Since we had started the conversation as a research project, people were already thinking about the topic. We were able to research reactions to our marketing message, and once the announcement was public, help build awareness.

You've Got Questions, LinkedIn Has Answers

LinkedIn Answers is a place to ask questions and get answers from anyone in the LinkedIn population; so unlike groups, you can potentially get a larger response.

Another way to get answers to your questions is to use a LinkedIn Poll (see Figure 1). In addition to showing up on LinkedIn, you can embed the poll on other sites.

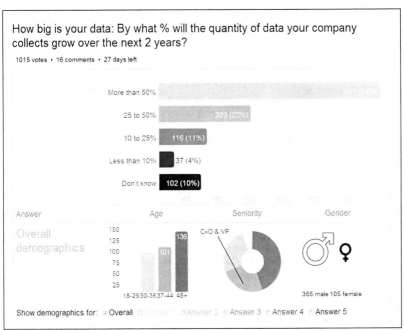

Figure 1: Results of a LinkedIn poll

When researching opinions, LinkedIn is a great substitute for a focus group.

2 Make a Good Tweet

Listen before you tweet, so that you understand the tone and dynamics of the conversation you are about to enter.

While it is easy to set up a Twitter account, it is an art to create high quality Twitter content that attracts a following and creates influence.

Of course, it is a matter of opinion what makes a good tweet, but there are some qualitative and quantitative measures that have been time tested and create a certain level of objectivity when judging a tweet.

How to create and identify a good tweet

Planning

- Listen before you tweet, so that you understand the tone and dynamics of the conversation you are about to enter.
- Provide good content. Whether you are sharing an original thought or a URL to an asset, make sure the content is audience appropriate and not a product pitch.
- Express that you are a person and not a corporation. Use simple language versus "marketing speak." If you are using a corporate account, identify yourself with your initials at the end of the tweet.
- Add your own insights versus just retweeting somebody else where possible.

Tweeting

- Make sure your tweet is not a one-off but a piece in a well-defined social media strategy that conveys a consistent story.
- Use established hashtags but not more than two at a time. Use them in context and not all at the end.

- Use only 120 characters or less so that a retweeter does not have to spend time modifying your tweet.
- If you tweet during an event, use the hashtag in all tweets.
- Don't just send URLs without context; they will look like spam.

Measuring impact

- Monitor that your tweet is retweeted by influencers and your target audience and not just by your friends and family.
- Ensure that the right people are following you, i.e., your target audience instead of focusing only on the total number.
- Collect anecdotal evidence that people enjoy your tweets.

You are on track when

- Your tweet is retweeted.
- People comment on your tweet.
- Your tweet achieves high reach in terms of impressions. The premise is that influencers have a large following and will influence your target audience.
- The click-through rate on URLs is high (e.g., via bit.ly).
- The number of followers increases consistently.
- Your Klout score or similar score increases and stays high.

Remember that content is king as on all social media channels. So make your tweets catchy to entice your audience to get engaged, e.g., ask them relevant questions.

Send only 5–10 tweets per day, well spaced out, and not in a rapid-fire fashion. That's a sure way to lose followers. Do some research on when your target audience is most active on Twitter. Then schedule your tweets to send them at the right time. SocialBro, Crowdbooster, and Buffer are some of the tools that can help you find the right time to tweet and help space them out.

If you don't have your Twitter account set up properly, it is highly unlikely that you will succeed on Twitter, no matter what you communicate. At a minimum, you need to have a professional picture or brand logo on your account, as well as a profile that states clearly who you are and your purpose on Twitter.

Free tools like Klout, Twittalyzer, and TweetReach are useful to help monitor your performance and fine-tune your Twitter interactions.

3 Build Your (Personal) Brand

"I have been reluctant to get into social media but you have convinced me, as I will be doing it for myself."

People are generally motivated by their own personal goals, not company goals. They want to earn money, solve interesting problems, or gain status. The same is true for their social media engagement.

When I (Natascha) hold social media workshops, there is usually a turning point when people realize that social media is their opportunity to make a name for themselves versus just taking on another project.

After a presentation I recently gave on the topic at a Global 2000 software company, multiple audience members approached me saying, "I have been reluctant to get into social media but you have convinced me, as I will be doing it for myself."

Social media is very democratic; you too can be an influencer. If you fill a void with your content and actively build your presence, you can establish yourself as an expert.

Why would a business care about the engagement of their employees on social media? First, it's better for employees to gain experience using their own social media channels than corporate ones. Second, if employees are knowledgeable in the use of social media, they can better support corporate programs.

In many cases, social media savvy employees will become brand ambassadors for their companies. They use their personal social channels to build a reputation by touting their expertise around their employer's products or services. Most large companies have several well-known product evangelists that are active in social media.

The steps to building a personal brand on social media are simple but require discipline and consistency.

Before you start

- Be clear about your objectives. Is your goal to create a presence related to your work expertise, or around a personal passion?
- Google yourself. Are you portraying the image you want to portray to customers, employers, and friends?
- What does success look like? Make it as tangible as possible so that you can measure and adapt.
- Who is your target audience? If you have multiple audiences, be sure that they have converging interests; at least enough to ensure that all your messages are relevant to all the people who will follow your channel(s). Otherwise, set up separate accounts for personal vs. professional interests.
- Do you know on which social channels your audience gets their information and engages? If your audience does not use Twitter, then there is no point for you to be there.

Once you start your social media presence

- Make sure you have enough of the right content. Create an editorial calendar to keep yourself on track. For example, the CMO of a large software company requires people on his staff to create a pipeline of at least five blog posts before they can start blogging. And ideas for five more after that.
- Your profiles on social media sites are equivalent to your business card in the physical world, so take care in creating a consistent and recognizable presence. Avoid using your employer's name in your channel name (for example, Twitter handle), or you might have to rebuild your presence if you change jobs.
- Convey a consistent message on all social media channels that you use; of course targeted to each medium but telling one coherent story overall.
- Engage regularly, and tweet once a day at a minimum, post a blog once a week, and post on Facebook every few days.
- Have a personality. People are tired of "bots" (automated tweeters) and corporate-sounding promotions.
- Use social media's true advantage: the fact that you can engage one-on-one. Reply when people comment on your blogs, add insightful comments when you retweet, and build relationships and a good reputation along the way.

4 Use Social Media for Internal Marketing

As employees tire of email volume, social media can keep people informed and engaged.

Social media is not just for interacting with your customers or prospects. Innovative companies use social media techniques internally to enhance communications, foster collaboration, and enrich their culture.

Communications

In large corporations with many products, you may need to internally market a product before or concurrently with your external launch.

Many people acknowledge the limitations of email as the primary form of corporate communication. Instant messaging, text messaging, or micro-blogging usually provide much faster replies, especially if the information exchange requirements are relatively modest.

An individual email represents an inherently outbound-only communication, as opposed to the dialogue paradigm that generally characterizes social media. Using a social platform, managers can initiate a conversation, possibly via a short email, by pointing people to content on internal blogs or communities, where they can add their own opinions, which are captured in a more obvious threaded manner.

Using social platforms for internal marketing has the added advantage that it allows sales teams to ask questions and talk to each other about the advantages of the new product or updated version. Further, the posts will remain archived to serve as a repository of training information, demos, proof of concepts, and customer references.

Collaboration

The key to success in generating online collaboration is to match interested people with relevant content. Your members must know where conversations are taking place and how to participate in them by adding their own content. While building an intelligent taxonomy helps, site navigation becomes more important when the scope of the site exceeds its original charter. This is common when a community becomes very successful and adds new content areas.

Use Case—Frequently Asked Questions

My (Peter's) product marketing team used wikis extensively to share information about our products. We built lists of frequently asked questions that were updated in near real-time by the technical experts. The ease of updating a wiki compared to the traditional corporate portals made it the first stop for posting timely information for sales reps. Further, sales reps could make updates as they succeeded in deals. The flexibility in formatting and hyperlinking to other pages made it preferable to any other method of sharing information.

Use Case—Culture

At one large software company, there are many active online communities in which different internal groups share information with each other and the rest of the organization. For example, the chief marketing officer (CMO) posts organizational announcements, information about corporate programs, and various musings about how he sees marketing. This is in lieu of blasting everyone with emails on those topics. This allows everyone to comment, ask questions, and join the conversation.

Employees are encouraged to write; some discuss programs they are working on, others summarize major customer events, and others start conversations about best practices. In many cases, comments from peers and management form a rich discussion around the topics.

Going Social

- Think about how you communicate with your employees and peers and how to make it a conversation versus "talking at them."
- Use the wisdom of experts within your organization to make better business decisions that leverage collective knowledge and experience.
- Leverage social media technologies to speed decision making.

"If HP knew what HP knows, we'd be three times more profitable", is a famous quote by Lew Platt, former CEO of HP. This can be the value you get out of using social media internally.

5 Extend Live Events with Mobile Apps

For every attendee you have on-site at your event, there are many more that could not make the trip.

In your B2B marketing efforts, you may have already built mobile apps or are currently planning for a new app. By integrating your social media efforts into an established mobile app that supports your brand, you can take advantage of a marketing vehicle that attracts highly social brand ambassadors.

B2B apps that are created specifically for use at in-person events such as trade shows and conferences are primed for multiple uses of social media. Attendees at these events can use the brand's mobile app to interact with one another and share ideas and information with virtual attendees.

Here are some ideas to include in your mobile events apps:

Connect: Give attendees the ability to connect with each other through their choice of social interface. This can be done using popular social platforms like LinkedIn, Facebook, and Google+, by connecting with their publicly available APIs within your events app. A simple listing of attendees at your event with profile information and photos can constitute an invitation to connect, increasing the value of the mobile app at your event.

Share: For every attendee you have on-site at your event, there are many more that could not make the trip. Turn your attendees into potential ambassadors by providing the ability to share information from your event in real-time through those social platforms they are most familiar with. Each piece of content within your app should include a social sharing functionality that will send out a short description of the content with a link back to the HTML version of your content.

Feedback: Take advantage of real-time feedback from your event attendees with instant reviews and comments built into your mobile app. The feedback can be as simple as a one through five star rating, or more complex and specific "like" ratings for content, speaker presentations, logistics, and more. Qualitative responses can help you hone your presentations when your attendees have the opportunity to send in direct feedback. Finally, you may choose to enable a threaded discussion within the app platform that allows attendees to share ideas and converse about content and structure.

Compete: Gamification (see Rule 12, "Add Gamification") in mobile applications is a natural fit. Making the app more fun and allowing people to compete against others can lead to increased adoption of the app. You can use simple competition within the app to encourage specific actions and behaviors. For instance, if you want to encourage the sharing of photos within the app, you can offer a higher point-value for that action. Likewise, sharing content with other social platforms would be a high-value action. Where simple actions such as "liking" comments or posting one- to five-word comments would not gain the attendee more than just a few points. Keep in mind that you will see some attendees skyrocket to the top of the leaderboard by completing actions just to be the leader. Prepare your rules and prizes accordingly.

Appendices

The appendices contain additional information you can use to become more effective at using social media to generate real business results.

- Appendix A: Key Social Media Sites
- Appendix B: Useful Social Media Tools
- Appendix C: Recommended Reading

Appendix

A Key Social Media Sites

Key Social Media Sites

Tool	URL	Description
LinkedIn	http://LinkedIn.com/	Business networking
Facebook	http://facebook.com/	Social networking
Twitter	http://twitter.com/	Microblogging
SlideShare	http://slideshare.net/	Presentation sharing
Google+	http://plus.google.com/	Social networking
Pinterest	http://pinterest.com/	Virtual pinboard for images
YouTube	http://YouTube.com/	Video sharing

B | Useful Social Media Tools

Twitter Tools

Tool	URL	Description
TwitterFeed	http://twitterfeed.com/	Converts RSS feeds to tweets
TwitterCounter	http://twittercounter.com/	Statistics for a Twitter account
Tweet2Tweet	http://tweet2tweet.appspot.com/	Shows the conversation between two Twitter accounts
TweetReach	http://tweetreach.com/	Shows accounts reached and impressions for a Twitter account or tweet
HootSuite	http://hootsuite.com/	Social media management system
SocialBro	http://www.socialbro.com/	Analysis of your Twitter account
Twitalyzer	http://twitalyzer.com/	Analysis of your Twitter account

Social Media Intelligence and Sentiment Analysis Tools

Tool	URL	Description
Social Mention	http://www.socialmention.com/	Real-time social media search and analysis
Addictomatic	http://addictomatic.com/	Create custom page from social media sites on a topic
People Browser	http://www.peoplebrowsr.com/	Social analytics
Crowdbooster	http://crowdbooster.com/	Social analytics
Radian6	http://www.radian6.com/	Social media listening, monitoring, and engagement
Sysomos	http://www.sysomos.com/	Social media listening and sentiment analysis
NetBase	http://netbase.com/	Social media listening and sentiment analysis
Visible	http://www.visibletechnologies.com/	Social media listening and sentiment analysis
SAS	http://bit.ly/b2bmkt-ab01[35]	Social media listening and sentiment analysis
Autonomy	http://promote.autonomy.com/	Social media listening and sentiment analysis

35. www.sas.com/software/customer-intelligence/social-media-analytics/

Pinterest Tools

Tool	URL	Description
Pinpuff	http://pinpuff.com/	Calculate your pinfluence
Pinreach	http://www.pinreach.com/	Pinterest influence & analytics

Other Tools

Tool	URL	Description
Google Alerts	http://alerts.google.com/	Alerts on saved Google searches
Awareness Hub	http://www.awarenessnetworks.com/	Social media publishing
Spredfast	http://www.spredfast.com/	Social media publishing
Curata	http://www.curata.com/	Curation and publishing
Klout	http://klout.com/	Influence scores
Kred	http://kred.com/	Influence scores
PeerIndex	http://www.peerindex.com/	Influence scores
Bit.ly	http://bit.ly/	URL shortener with statistics
Trackur	http://www.trackur.com/	Influence scores
AddToAny	http://share.lockerz.com/	Social sharing
AddThis	http://www.addthis.com/	Social sharing
ShareThis	http://sharethis.com/	Social sharing

C Recommended Reading and Podcasts

Books

- *Groundswell*—Charlene Li, Josh Bernoff
- *New Rules of Marketing and PR*—David Meerman Scott
- *Social Marketing to the Business Customer*—Paul Gillin, Eric Schwartzman
- *Measure What Matters: Online Tools For Understanding Customers, Social Media, Engagement, and Key Relationships*—Katie Delahaye Paine
- *eMarketing Strategies for the Complex Sale*—Ardath Albee
- *Content Rules*—Ann Handley, C. C. Chapman
- *Crowdsourcing: Why the Power of the Crowd Is Driving the Future of Business*—Jeff Howe

Blogs

- B2B Marketing Insider
  http://www.b2bmarketinginsider.com/
- B2B Social Media Marketing
  http://www.MarketingXLerator.com
- Britopian—Insights from Michael Brito
  http://www.britopian.com/
- Business2Community
  http://www.business2community.com/
- Chief Marketing Technologist
  http://chiefmartec.com/
- Forbes Social Media
  http://www.forbes.com/social-media/
- Mashable
  http://mashable.com/
- The Daily SEO Blog
  http://www.seomoz.org/blog
- Smartblog on Social Media
  http://smartblogs.com/category/social-media/

- Social Media and Technology
  http://mprocopio.com/blog
- Social Media Examiner
  http://www.socialmediaexaminer.com/
- Social Media B2B
  http://socialmediab2b.com/
- thinkJar
  http://estebankolsky.com/
- WebInkNow
  http://www.webinknow.com/
- Web Strategist Blog
  http://www.web-strategist.com/blog/

Podcasts

- Marketing Over Coffee, weekly about 20 minutes
  http://www.marketingovercoffee.com/
- For Immediate Release, weekly about one hour plus interviews, speeches, and book reviews
  http://forimmediaterelease.biz/
- On the Record Online, interviews with social media leaders and practitioners
  http://ontherecordpodcast.com/pr/otro/default.aspx

About the Authors

Michael Procopio has more than 25 years' experience in high-tech organizations as a business leader and technology and marketing manager. As a social media strategist he consults with companies from small to Fortune 1000 on social media and social intelligence. Previously he managed HP Software's overall social media presence and direction where a social media lead gen activity yielded a 2500+% ROI. Michael speaks internationally about social media and is a member of the Society for New Communications Research, IEEE, and was in the HP Digital Marketing Council and is an HP trained Wikipedian. Michael holds a BS in Computer Science and Electrical Engineering from California State University, Long Beach. He resides along California's Central Coast. Learn more at http://mprocopio.com.

Peter Spielvogel has been a high-tech marketing executive since the early 1990s and a business-to-business social media practitioner since 2005. Peter uses social media extensively to understand market requirements, build awareness among current and future customers, engage in online discussions, promote events, and generate targeted leads. He leverages wikis to share fresh content among marketing, sales, product management, and various technical teams. In his current role at SAP, he provides product marketing and product management expertise to a customer-focused development group. Previously, at HP, he led a global product marketing team. Prior to HP, he held executive-level marketing roles at several startup companies. Peter's education includes an MBA from the Tuck School of Business at Dartmouth and a BS in Engineering from Princeton University. He is based in Silicon Valley, California.

Natascha Thomson has over 15 years' experience in B2B marketing with a focus on using social media to connect people for business since 2007. She is the founder and owner of MarketingXLerator, a B2B social media marketing consultancy. In this role, she is able to draw from her background in online community marketing, competitive intelligence, partner marketing, analyst relations, product marketing, and product management. Most recently, as an executive at SAP, Natascha provided social media consulting and training for SAP organizations, including strategy development and ROI measurement. She has worked in Europe and the USA at startups and large corporations, including HP and EMC. Natascha's education includes an Executive MBA from St. Mary's College of California, and a Master of Commerce and Arts from the University of Passau, Germany. She lives in Silicon Valley, California. Learn more at http://www.MarketingXLerator.com.

The authors are donating all their royalties to the Khan Academy, an organization committed to providing a free world-class education to anyone anywhere. The publisher is matching their contribution dollar for dollar.

Contributor:

Chad Summervill has over 10 years' experience in B2B digital marketing. He currently leads Enterprise Digital Engagement & Events for HP Marketing Strategy and Innovation. Chad works on digital programs including Enterprise Events Mobile Ecosystem which provides the vendor and its customers new ways to interact at large conferences and trade shows. Previously at HP, Chad has led B2B mobile programs and interactive marketing for HP Networking, Small and Medium Business, and the Public Sector. Chad holds an MBA from the University of Phoenix and a BA in Music from Western Washington University. He can be found in Boise, ID at a local coffee shop or at http://www.chadsummervill.com.

42 Rules Program

A lot of people would like to write a book, but only a few actually do. Finding a publisher, distributing, and marketing the book are challenges that prevent even the most ambitious authors from getting started.

If you want to be a successful author, we'll provide you the tools to help make it happen. Start today by completing a book proposal at our website http://42rules.com/write/.

For more information, email info@superstarpress.com or call 408-257-3000.

Other Happy About Books

42 Rules for Applying Google Analytics

This book is about understanding a visitor's journey through your website then applying that measurement, collection and analysis of data for the main purpose of adequately optimizing and improving website performance.

Paperback: $19.95
eBook: $14.95

#GOOGLE+ for BUSINESS tweet

In *#GOOGLE+ for BUSINESS tweet*, Janet walks you through the gamut of Google+ tools and techniques.

Paperback: $19.95
eBook: $14.95

Social Media Success!

This book is a launch pad for successful social media engagement. It shows how to identify the right networks, find the influencers, the people you want to talk to and which tools will work the best for you.

Paperback: $19.95
eBook: $14.95

I Need a Killer Press Release—Now What???

If you are a small to mid-size business owner who wants to understand online news promotion, or work for a PR firm who wants to add online optimization and SEO to your press releases, this book is written for you.

Paperback: $29.95
eBook: $14.95

Purchase these books at Happy About
http://happyabout.com/
or at other online and physical bookstores.

A Message From Super Star Press™

Thank you for your purchase of this 42 Rules Series book. It is available online at: http://happyabout.com/42rules/b2bsocialmediamarketing.php or at other online and physical bookstores. To learn more about contributing to books in the 42 Rules series, check out http://superstarpress.com.

Please contact us for quantity discounts at sales@superstarpress.com.

If you want to be informed by email of upcoming books, please email bookupdate@superstarpress.com.

CPSIA information can be obtained at www.ICGtesting.com
Printed in the USA
LVOW071417030113

314232LV00009B/127/P